FOR REFERENCE ONLY

PUBLIC RECORD OFFICE READERS' GUIDE NO. 1

HARTLEPOOL REFERENCE
124 YORK ROAD,
HARTLEPOOL, CLEVELAND.
TS26 9DE

D1362944

MAKING USE OF
THE CENSUS

BY

SUSAN LUMAS

929.341

0029130921

HARTLEPOOL BOROUGH LIBRARIES
HZ

0029130921   0029130921

ACKNOWLEDGEMENTS

Thanks are due to many people who helped with the compilation of this guide. Evelyn Goode input the text initially and subsequently took it through its many drafts to what you see before you. Melvyn Stainton was responsible for the painstaking transformation from typescript to illustrated book. I also owe a debt to many colleagues who have shared my enthusiasm for the Victorian censuses and who have sat behind the census room enquiry desk at one time or another: Joe Saunders, who taught me all I know; Andy Bodle, Nigel Kent and Gerry Toop, who contributed helpful advice; Amanda Bevan, Mandy Banton, John Post, David Crook, Elizabeth Hallam-Smith and Alfred Knightbridge, who guided a rough draft through many editorial metamorphoses to its present state; Hugh Ashley Rayner, who photographed the documents; and especially Edward Higgs, whose much greater knowledge of how and why the census was taken was always there to be tapped when necessary. Thanks are also due to the late Alan Reed who provided some useful information based on his considerable experience as a lecturer on the subject and, last but not least, to all those searchers, record agents and transcribers who pointed out interesting entries, who shared their experience and who asked the questions.

The provenance and date of the cover illustration are unknown. It is likely that it was used in a newspaper to publicise the imminent taking of the census.

PRO Publications
Public Record Office
Ruskin Avenue
Kew
Surrey
TW9 4DU

© Crown Copyright 1997
Third Edition

ISBN 1 873162 43 X

FAMILY RECORDS CENTRE - FIRST FLOOR PLAN

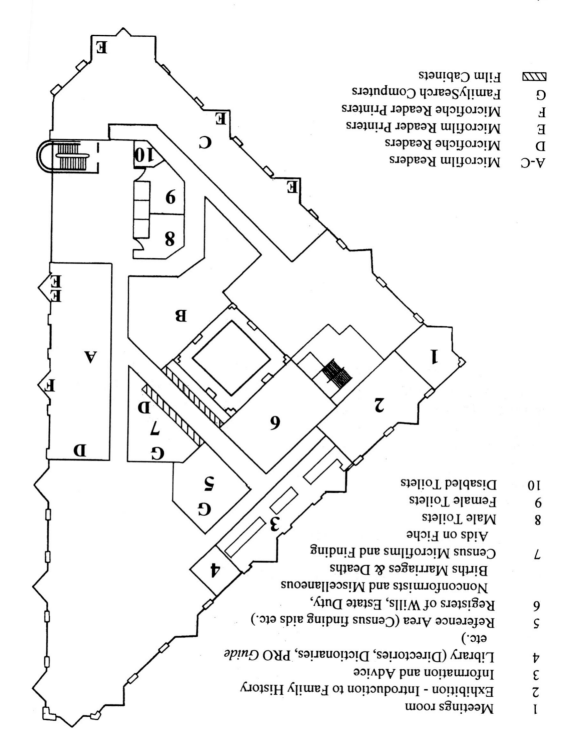

1   Meetings room
2   Exhibition - Introduction to Family History
3   Information and Advice
4   Library (Directories, Dictionaries, PRO Guide etc.)
5   Reference Area (Census finding aids etc.)
6   Registers of Wills, Estate Duty, Nonconformists and Miscellaneous Births Marriages & Deaths
7   Census Microfilms and Finding Aids on Fiche
8   Male Toilets
9   Female Toilets
10   Disabled Toilets

A-C   Microfilm Readers
D   Microfiche Readers
E   Microfilm Reader Printers
F   Microfiche Reader Printers
G   FamilySearch Computers
     Film Cabinets

LOCATION PLAN - FAMILY RECORDS CENTRE

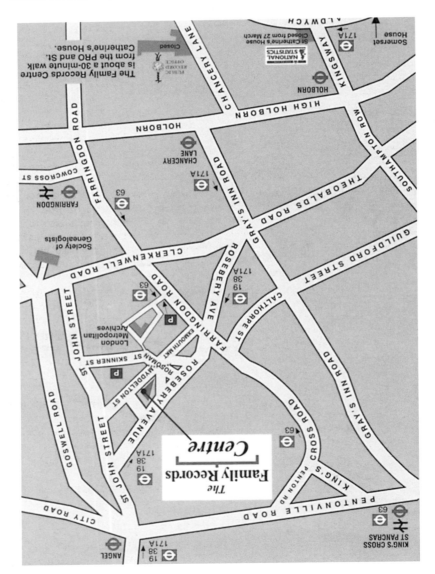

Family Records Centre, 1 Myddelton Street, London EC1R 1UW.
Telephone: 0181 392 5300.

Opening hours: Monday, Wednesday and Friday 9 am to 5 pm
Tuesday 10 am to 7 pm
Thursday 9 am to 7 pm
Saturday 9.30 am to 5 pm

ILLUSTRATIONS

CONTENTS

INTRODUCTION

The purpose of this readers' guide is to help researchers to find their way into the nineteenth century census returns held by the Public Record Office (PRO). Whether they are seeking to compare occupations in a particular suburb of an industrial town over a thirty-year period, or to search for an individual in the course of piecing together a family history, it will give them guidance in understanding and interpreting this significant and fascinating source. It explains how to cope with the census reading rooms at the Family Records Centre, and how to use the PRO's finding aids to identify the relevant microfilm (the medium by which these records are made available). It should be of value to those consulting census microfilms held outside the PRO, in local record offices and libraries, because it clarifies the structure of the census and also deals with a variety of problems encountered by its readers (eg how to locate a particular place or to seek a missing house).

The ideal enumerator

'A person of intelligence and activity, he must read and write well and have some knowledge of arithmetic. He must not be infirm or of such weak health as may render him unable to undergo the requisite exertion. He should not be younger than 18 years or older than 65 years. He must be temperate, orderly and respectable and be such a person as is likely to conduct himself with strict propriety and deserve the good will of the inhabitants of his district.'

The ideal householder

'*The schedule should be received with intelligent acquiescence, and filled up with the persuasion that the integrity and enlightenment of all are tacitly challenged to take a conscientious share fulfilling a truly important duty.*'

The Caernarfon and Denbigh Herald, 1871

MAKING USE OF THE CENSUS

The nineteenth century census returns provide a fascinating field of study and a valuable introduction to the use of archives. Many people might not need to look at original documents until their studies point them first in the direction of the enumerators' returns and all they have to offer; but they will soon find that the returns provide a rich source for many areas of research: from general population studies of an economic or social nature, through research into particular localities, to studies of individuals by family historians and biographers. It is not possible, however, just to walk into a reading room to find an index designed for your exact purpose that will lead you straight to the particular page, or pages, of the census returns that you require. Archives are left in the order in which they remained after their immediate administrative use was over, which tells us something of how they were compiled and administered. They have not been rearranged to suit the potential user, because today's researcher may not be seeking the same information as a reader of one hundred years hence.

WHAT THERE IS AND WHERE TO FIND IT

A census of Great Britain has been taken every decade from 1801 onwards, with the exception of 1941 when war intervened. The results were digested and published as Parliamentary Papers, to provide population counts (see appendix 1) and other social statistics for immediate use. For a detailed study of how and why the census was taken see E J Higgs, *Making Sense of the Census* and *A Clearer Sense of the Census* (see bibliography appendix 11).

The earlier returns, for 1801 to 1831, were simply a numerical count and give little detailed information except where an enumerator decided to exceed his duties and include more. These returns have not been officially preserved but some survive locally, often in county record offices. The whereabouts of such survivals may be discovered by consulting J S W Gibson's *Marriage, Census and other Indexes for Family Historians*, and C R Chapman's *Pre 1841 Censuses and Population Listings*.

From 1841, however, all the enumerators' returns, but not the original schedules, have been officially preserved in theory, although in practice not all have survived. It was realised that these returns could usefully serve purposes other than those intended by the original survey.

The returns for England and Wales, which include the Isle of Man and the Channel Islands (referred to as Islands in the British Seas), the Isle of Wight (returned with Hampshire), and the Scilly Isles (returned with Cornwall), for 1841 to 1891 (HO 107, RG 9 to RG 12) are available on microfilm, and for 1891 also on microfiche, for public inspection at the

HM Napoleon III Emperor of the French RG 10/876, f 14 p 82

Family Records Centre, Myddelton Street, London EC1R 1UW (telephone 0181 392 5300). The census reading rooms are open between 9.00 am and 5.00 pm on Monday, Wednesday and Friday, 10.00 am - 7.00 pm on Tuesday, 9.30 am - 5.00 pm on Saturday and 9.00 am - 7.00 pm on Thursday.

Copies are also available in some local record offices and libraries (see J S W Gibson's *Census Returns 1841 - 1881 on Microfilm*). In the United States of America, copies on microfilm of all returns are held by The Genealogical Society of Utah, 50 East North Temple, Salt Lake City, Utah 84150.

The returns are, however, subject to a one hundred year closure period because of the personal information which they contain. One hundred years means one hundred years, not ninety-nine years and a half; the census returns, having usually been taken in April, are opened after their closure period on the first working day of the following year. For the dates of census night for each year see appendix 1.

The 1901 census for England and Wales, which is still in the custody of the Registrar General, may be consulted for information on a person's age and place of birth only, if you are a direct descendant of the individual or individuals whose details you require, or next of kin, where the person has died childless, by applying on a special form to the Office for National Statistics, Room 4324, Segensworth Road, Titchfield, Hampshire, PO15 5RR, for a search to be made. Because of the stricter assurances of confidentiality than for earlier censuses given at that time it is not yet possible to do the same for 1911. Also the returns for that year were not entered into enumerators' books, so a search of the original schedules which are retained in place of the books would present considerable difficulties.

The Scottish returns are held at the General Register Office for Scotland, New Register House, Edinburgh EH1 3YT (telephone 0131 556 395).

Irish returns rarely survive before 1901. *Handbook on Irish Genealogy*, published by Heraldic Artists Ltd., Dublin lists, on p 39, those census records which have survived in the National Archives in Dublin for some counties. Begley's *Irish Genealogy: A Record Finder* (p 51), has a comprehensive survey of Irish census returns from as far back as 1630 to 1981, and a full list of what has survived. These two lists are not identical.

Censuses were also taken in many British colonies on the same dates as those for the UK, but little information other than the purely statistical exists for them in this country. There is, however, a census of convicts in New South Wales and Tasmania, 1788 to 1859, in HO 10/21-27; an 1811 census of Surinam (CO 278/15-25); a 1715 census of Barbados but only of the white population (CO 28/16); and a census of Sierra Leone for 1831 (CO 267/111).

John Cadbury Cocoa Manufacturer   RG 9/2124, f 4 p 2

ARRANGEMENT OF THE RECORDS

The census returns are arranged topographically (that is, by place) in the order in which they appear in the published tables. The arrangement follows the system used for the registration of births, marriages and deaths. In 1836, when civil registration was established, the poor law unions were used as a foundation for the boundaries of the registration districts. The superintendent registrar's districts, grouped into eleven divisions, were also used as administrative units for census taking and were numbered. The divisions are described in appendix 2. The returns appear in numerical order of registration district. Later legislation altered the boundaries of the superintendent registrar's districts in order to confine individual districts within county boundaries which hitherto some had straddled. Some places, therefore, moved from one district to another as later censuses were taken. See appendix 5 for a complete list of registration districts and their numbers.

Each superintendent registrar's district is divided into sub-districts, and each sub-district into enumeration districts. The enumeration districts vary in size. Those covering a rural area took into account the distance that one man could travel in a day to collect the schedules from each household. On the other hand, enumeration districts in large towns, with a greater concentration of people, cover a much smaller area on the ground but a much larger number of individuals. Parishes, townships, tithings, hamlets and liberties are gathered into appropriate enumeration districts, which may consist of several small places or an entire parish. In other cases there may be several enumeration districts covering one large parish. It is important to remember that these parishes are civil parishes and do not necessarily have the same boundaries as their ecclesiastical equivalents.

The civil parish was the result of poor law administration which in itself created boundary problems. The ecclesiastical parishes, which were based on the ancient parishes of England and Wales together with chapelries created when the population increased and needed more places of worship, were found to be too large and unwieldy for administrative purposes and individual townships or tithings and villages were allowed to levy their own rates. This resulted in the establishment of civil parishes, as distinct from ecclesiastical districts or parishes, especially during the nineteenth century. In 1871 the ancient parishes which had not already been sub-divided into chapelries and townships were renamed as civil parishes. In addition there were extra-parochial places called liberties, or simply termed extra-parochial. All of these sub-divisions are mentioned in the population tables; the ecclesiastical districts are in separate sections at the end of each region. For census searching, however, ecclesiastical districts are usually ignored and the civil parish is the unit which matters.

James A H Murray Lexicographer RG 12/1166 , f 65 p 3

5

HOW THE CENSUS WAS TAKEN

In the week preceding census night (see appendix 1 for the date of each census) the appointed enumerator delivered schedules (see pp 7 and 8) to all the households in the area to which he had been assigned. The schedule was a form that every householder was obliged to complete. A householder was anyone who rented or owned a dwelling, a lodger being a householder if he or she lived in the same building but had separate accommoda-tion from the rest of the people living there. A boarder was someone who lived with the householder's family and shared their dining table, unlike a lodger who occupied a separate household (see p 55) for a boarder and a lodger under one roof). Everyone who slept in the house on census night was to be included, even if it was not their permanent home. The instructions to the enumerator were that no person present on that night was to be omitted, and no person absent included. If individuals were working that night, or were travelling, they would be enumerated in the house to which they would normally return on the morning after they had finished their shift, or where they were to stay at the next stop on their journey.

> *ENUMERATOR'S REMARKS FROM 1851 CENSUS FOR LONDON*
>
> *ALL HALLOWS, BARKING, LONDON*
>
> *The enumeration of this district was undertaken by me in the belief that I should be fairly paid for my services.*
>
> *I was not aware that all the particulars were to be entered by the enumerator in a book, the work without that, being ample for the sum paid, nor had I any idea of the unreasonable amount of labour imposed. The distribution, collection etc of the schedules together with the copying of the same occupied from two or three hours for every sixty persons enumerated, and for that - the equivalent is - ONE SHILLING!!!*
>
> *What man possessing the intelligence and business habits necessary for the undertaking would be found to accept it, if aware of the labour involved. How then can a correct return of the population be expected?*
>
> *He who proposed the scale of remuneration, should, in justice, be compelled to enumerate a large district, such as this upon the terms he had himself fixed.*
>
> *HO 107/1531 f 193*

On the Monday after the census night the enumerator returned to collect the completed schedules. If any had not been filled in, the enumerator had to do so by asking the householder for the information.

John Poyntz, Earl and Groom to the Prince Consort RG 9/949, f 32 p 19

GENERAL INSTRUCTION.

This Paper to be filled up by the OCCUPIER or person in charge of the dwelling.

If a house is let or sub-let to separate Families or Lodgers, each OCCUPIER or LODGER must make a return for his portion of the house upon a SEPARATE PAPER.

INSTRUCTIONS for filling up the Column headed "RANK, PROFESSION, or OCCUPATION."

A person following more Distinct Occupations than one, should insert them in the order of their importance.

1. The superior Titles of PEERS and other PERSONS OF RANK to be inserted, as well as any important Office they may hold.
2. MEMBERS OF PARLIAMENT, MAGISTRATES, Aldermen, and other important public Officers, to state their profession or occupation, if any, after their official rank or title.
3. All persons serving in the ARMY AND NAVY, to state their rank and the branch of the service to which they belong. Officers to state whether on the Active or Retired List; Chelsea, Greenwich, and other Pensioners, to be so designated.
4. All persons in the CIVIL SERVICE to state their rank, and the department to which they belong; those retired or superannuated to be distinguished.
5. MINISTERS OF RELIGION.—Clergymen of the Church of England to return themselves as "Rector of ——," "Vicar of ——," "Curate of ——," &c., or as "retired Clergyman of the Church of England."

13. AGRICULTURAL LABORERS, SHEPHERDS and others employed on Farms, but not living in the Farmer's house, must be described as *Agricultural Laborers, Shepherds*, &c.
14. PERSONS ENGAGED IN COMMERCE as Merchants, Brokers, Agents, &c., to state in all cases the particular branch of Commerce in which they are engaged.
15. In TRADES, MANUFACTURES, or other Business, Masters must, in all cases, be distinguished.
16. WORKERS IN MANUFACTURES or MINES.
17. ENGINEERS.—Civil Engineers to be so described.
18. ARTISANS AND MECHANICS.
20. DOMESTIC SERVANTS.
21. MESSENGERS, PORTERS, LABORERS.
22. PERSONS FOLLOWING NO PROFESSION, TRADE, OR CALLING.
24. WOMEN AND CHILDREN.

CENSUS OF ENGLAND AND WALES, 1871.

HOUSEHOLDER'S SCHEDULE.

Prepared under the direction of one of Her Majesty's Principal Secretaries of State, pursuant to the Act of 33 and 34 Vict., c. 107.

No. 190

Parish or Township	Sheffield
City, Town, or Village	Sheffield
Street, Square, &c., or Road	Victoria Street
Name of Occupier, and No. of House	51 — Vaughan

TO THE OCCUPIER.

You are requested to insert the particulars specified on the other side, in compliance with an Act which passed the House of Commons, and the House of Lords, in the last Session of Parliament, and received the assent of Her Majesty The Queen on the 10th of August, 1870.

This Paper will be CALLED FOR on MONDAY, APRIL 3rd, by the appointed Enumerator,

Approved.
H. A. BRUCE,
Home Office, Whitehall, Nov. 17th, 1870.

GEORGE GRAHAM,
Registrar General.

THREE EXAMPLES of the MODE OF FILLING UP THE HOUSEHOLDER'S SCHEDULE.

	Name and Surname	Relation to Head of Family	Condition	Sex	Age (last Birthday)	Rank, Profession, or Occupation	Where Born	If (1) Deaf-and-Dumb (2) Blind (3) Imbecile or Idiot (4) Lunatic
1st Example	1 George Wood	Head of Family	Married	M.	48	Farmer of 317 acres, employing 8 labourers and 3 boys	Surrey, Godstone	
	2 Maria Wood	Wife	Married	F.	44	Farmer's Wife	Scotland	
	3 Alan Wood	Son	Unmarried	M.	20	Farmer's Son	Surrey, Godstone	
	4 Flora Jane Wood	Daughter	Unmarried	F.	12	Scholar	Kent, Ramsgate	
	5 Ellen Wood	Mother	Widow	F.	71	Annuitant	Canada	
	6 Eliza Edwards	Servant	Unmarried	F.	24	General Servant (Domestic)	Middlesex, Paddington	
	7 Ann Young	Servant	Unmarried	F.	22	Dairymaid	Surrey, Croydon	
	8 Thomas Jones	Servant	Unmarried	M.	21	Farm Servant	Essex, Epping	Lunatic.
2nd Example	1 Janet Cox	Head of Family	Widow	F.	49	Staymaker	Scotland	
	2 William Cox	Son	Unmarried	M.	18	Basket-maker	Surrey, Lambeth	
	3 Sophia Cox	Daughter	Unmarried	F.	15	Dressmaker	Middlesex, Poplar	
	4 Alexander Cox	Grandson		M.	11 months		Middlesex, Shoreditch	
	5 Margaret Cox	Mother-in-law	Widow	F.	73	Formerly Laundress	Ireland	Blind from Small-pox.
	6 John Butler	Boarder	Widower	M.	42	Printer—Compositor	France (British Subject)	
3rd Example	1 Walter Johnson	Lodger	Unmarried	M.	23	Ship Carpenter	Durham, Sunderland	

BY AUTHORITY:—FORD and TILT, Long Acre, London, Printers to Her Majesty's Stationery Office.

Householder's schedule for Victoria Street, Sheffield.   RG 10/4677, f 76

LIST of the MEMBERS of this FAMILY, of VISITORS, of SERVANTS, and of ALL OTHER PERSONS, who SLEPT or ABODE in this Dwelling on the NIGHT of SUNDAY, APRIL 2nd, 1871.

No.	NAME and SURNAME	RELATION to Head of Family	CONDITION	AGE (Last Birthday)	SEX	RANK, PROFESSION, or OCCUPATION	WHERE BORN	If (1) Deaf-and-Dumb (2) Blind (3) Imbecile or Idiot (4) Lunatic
1	Bartlett Davis Wrangham	Head of Family	Married	44	M	Captain of Adjt. Sea Artillery	Yorkshire – Sheffield	
2	John Bartlett Wrangham	Son		6	M	Scholar	Yorkshire – Sheffield	
3	Sarah Wrangham	Sister	Unmarried	34	F	Housekeeper	Yorkshire – Sheffield	
4	James Watson	Visitor	Widower	74	M	Vicar of Man	Yorkshire – Harrogate	
5	Annie Elizabeth Hays	Servant	Unmarried	24	F	Cook		
6	Martha Jane Hays	Servant	Unmarried	14	F	Parlour Maid	Lancashire – Walmley	
7								
8			To be returned to the Census Office					
9								
10								
11								
12		Sheffield sub-District						
13			M	3				
14			F	3				
15								

I declare the foregoing to be a true Return, according to the best of my knowledge and belief.

Witness my Hand, (Signature) _____

Completed schedule for the Wrangham family.   RG 10/4677, f 76

The schedules were then copied by the enumerator into a book (several of which were bound together into folders) and handed in to the registrar who checked that everything was satisfactory.

SUPERINTENDENT REGISTRAR'S DISTRICT.		Area in Statute Acres.	HOUSES.						POPULATION.			
			1851.			1861.			Persons.		Males.	
Sub-district.	Parish, Township, or Place.		Inha-bited.	Un-inha-bited.	Build-ing.	Inha-bited.	Un-inha-bited.	Build-ing.	1851.	1861.	1851.	1861.
	495. TODMORDEN.											
1. HEBDEN BRIDGE	*Halifax, part of* Parish—ᵃ											
	Wadsworth - - Township	10080	957	166	–	923	158	2	4491	4141	2188	1995
	Erringden - - Township	2980	333	47	1	371	44	–	1004	1764	995	863
	Heptonstall - - ᵇ Township	5320	882	127	2	790	170	6	4177	3497	2017	1728
	Stansfield, *part of* ᶜ - ᵈ Township [viz., the Lower Third Division.]		353	95	3	320	98	2	1790	1424	901	694
2. TODMORDEN -	*Halifax, part of* Parish—ᵃ	} 5920 {										
	Stansfield, *part of* ᶜ - Township [viz., the Middle Third and Upper Third Division.]		1132	102	11	1351	62	16	5837	6750	2925	3286
	Langfield - - - Township	2620	752	41	55	890	35	10	3729	4391	1805	2149
	Rochdale, part of Parish—ᵉ											
	TODMORDEN and Walsden } Townp. (*Lancashire*)	–	1481	114	31	1790	67	57	7699	9146	3738	4455
	496. SADDLEWORTH.											
1. DELPH ᵇᵇ -	Saddleworth, *part of* † - Township (*part of Rochdale Parish.*ᵇ)	} 18280 {	1819	230	10	2048	169	11	9440	9754	4647	4754
2. UPPER MILL ᵇᵇ -	Saddleworth, *part of* (W) † Township (*part of Rochdale Parish.*ᵇ)		1548	105	18	1770	116	6	8359	8877	4190	4390
	497. HUDDERSFIELD.											
1. SLAITHWAITE -	*Huddersfield, part of* Parish—ᶜ											
	Slaithwaite - - Township	2320	553	29	7	575	11	2	2852	2932	1460	1465
	Marsden { in *Huddersfield* Parish ᶜ -	2050	103	9	6	138	14	–	512	662	273	310
	Tnp.† ᵈ { in *Almondbury* Parish § ᶜ -	5061	407	50	4	428	23	1	2153	2097	1091	1015
	Almondbury, part of Parish—§ ᶜ											
	Lingards - - - Township	500	159	4	–	149	4	–	811	783	405	373
	Linthwaite, *part of* ‖ - ᶠ Township	809	264	13	–	309	16	2	1355	1567	692	789
2. MELTHAM -	*Almondbury, part of* Parish—§ ᶜ											
	South Crosland - Township	1560	536	36	2	582	38	5	2784	2794	1392	1362
	Meltham - - - Township	4525	684	42	20	795	75	2	3758	4046	1794	1885
3. HONLEY -	*Almondbury, part of* Parish—§ ᶜ											
	Honley (W) - - ᵍ Township	2790	1077	35	17	987	186	3	5595	4686	2775	2225
	Netherthong - - Township	850	228	13	5	222	30	–	1207	1097	615	536
4. HOLMFIRTH -	*Almondbury, part of* Parish—§ ᶜ											
	Upperthong - - ʰ Township	710	459	22	7	543	21	2	2463	2690	1235	1306
	Austonley - - ⁱ Township	1760	373	18	4	363	38	–	2234	1901	1130	939
	Holme - - - Township	3990	140	1	2	141	13	–	849	807	451	417
	Kirkburton, part of Parish—ʲ											
	Cartworth, *part of* ** - ᵏ Township	–	446	19	6	456	21	1	2292	2249	1168	1143
	Wooldale, *part of* †† - ᵏ Township	–	657	36	11	668	54	–	3469	3195	1804	1624
5. NEWMILL -	*Kirkburton, part of* Parish—ʲ											
	Wooldale, *part of* †† - ᵏ Township	2370	393	26	2	411	20	2	2131	2124	1070	1033
	Cartworth, *part of* ** - ᵏ Township	2820	47	10	–	47	1	–	240	254	118	136
	Hepworth - - - Township	3370	270	15	2	276	23	–	1532	1530	795	790
	Fulstone - - - Township	1200	415	10	3	455	42	–	2257	2414	1177	1238

The books were then sent to the census office in Craig's Court, London where they were checked again. Finally, when all the information had been analysed it was published as a Parliamentary Paper in the form of a series of tables relating to various subjects and the original schedules were destroyed. The tables most used by searchers are the tables of population arranged by registration districts (see bibliography appendix 11). Copies are available in the Census Room on request.

From 1891 women too could act as enumerators; it will be interesting to see how many accepted the challenge (see p 54).

Henry Mackeson Alderman Brewer HO 107/1633, f 543 p 1

THE CENSUS READING ROOM

On arrival at the Family Records Centre, Myddelton Street, if you ask to see the census records you will be directed to the reading room on the first floor. You do not need a reader's ticket. As you enter the reading room you will be given a numbered pass (illustrated below) to hang round your neck. This allows you into the room and indicates where you find your seat by the number found on the tables in the reading area. It has to be returned whenever you leave this room. A plan of the reading room is on page vi.

If you prefer you may leave your coat and excess baggage in the locker room on the Lower Ground Floor before proceeding upstairs (£1 coin, refundable, required). The Office will not accept responsibility for loss or damage to personal property, so please watch any possessions taken in with you.

The lower ground floor also has plenty of space for eating and drinking when you need a break and a drinks vending machine, but you will have to give up your seat to do this and acquire another seat number when you return to the reading room. It has facilities for disabled readers and a baby changing room.

The first thing you need to do before looking at a microfilm is to consult the books in the reference area.

The reference books provide you with all the information you need to identify the specific reels of film necessary for your search.

The entrance area to the reading room has three desks on the left-hand side. The first is where you are assigned a seat number which is on the pass you are asked to wear whilst using the room. The second is where you can make enquiries and the third is where you get help with the microfilm and microfiche readers and the photocopy machines.

Gabriel Rozetti Professor of Italian HO 107/12493, f 130 p 13

Opposite the desks are the shelves containing the reference books which are grouped by census year and bound in different colours. 1841 in green, 1851 in red, 1861 in blue, 1871 in brown, 1881 in cream and 1891 in white. They are described in greater detail below on page 13 but are summarised here. In this area you will also find nearly all of the surname indexes compiled by family history societies who often regard the Public Record Office, Society of Genealogists and the Family History Library at Salt Lake City as a place of deposit; PRO staff are always pleased to receive them. The filing drawers contain printed surname indexes, where they exist. There are some early indexes in typewritten format bound on the bookshelves and some later ones on microfiche. All finding aids on microfiche are conveniently to hand on a table by the microfiche readers immediately beyond the reference area.

On the shelves, grouped by the years of the census, you will find:

An index to places
A class list which gives you the film references (also called a reference book)
Street indexes to London and other large towns

On another set of shelves is a collection of further miscellaneous finding aids which help if any queries arise. They are:

copies of London street directories for the census years
    (also with colour-coded bindings)
three volumes that locate London streets
a list of ecclesiastical parishes
an index to 1861 shipping
an 1854 map of London

Additionally, there are five volumes which help clarify the whereabouts of London streets and a volume that explains the changes in county boundaries and civil parishes during the nineteenth century. There is also an alphabetical index to registration districts which gives a list of churches and chapels in each. There are other printed works available adjacent to the reference area which may help you, such as street directories and other general works.

Thomas Boozey Music Publisher HO 107/662, book 4 f 9 p 9

The PRO also makes available, on microfiche and now on CD-ROM, a copy of the International Genealogical Index (IGI) to enable people with an interest in individuals to ascertain in which county or counties a particular name is dominant. Once a successful search has been made for a family or an individual, a glance at the IGI will enlarge a searcher's knowledge of the spread of a particular surname in the county of birthplaces found in the census. It may even lead you to the specific reference in a parish or nonconformist register, as the IGI is an index to all the nonconformist registers held at the PRO and to many parish registers or parts of parish registers from all over the country.

FamilySearch on CD-ROM, is a collection of databases holding genealogical information which includes the International Genealogical Index and Ancestral File, a database of genealogies sent in to the Church of Jesus Christ of Latter Day Saints by people throughout the world. Use is limited to one hour at busy periods and there are no facilities to print from it.

The section on finding aids which follows explains in more detail how to use the reference area. They are a self-service operation although the staff are there to assist should you get into difficulties.

The cabinets holding the films are at the entrance to the part of the search room where you find the microfilm and microfiche readers.

In the area containing the microfilm readers there are reader printers which enable you to obtain photocopies of successful searches from film or fiche. This is a self-service facility: see p 58 and p 59 which show you how to use a reader-printer and p 57 describing how to identify the particular part of the film you wish to copy.

Drinking, eating and the chewing of gum are forbidden in all parts of the Census Room. When you need a break, please eat and drink in the refreshment room provided on the lower ground floor. Smoking is forbidden throughout the building.

William Wisden Cricket Outfitter RG 11/1088, f 16 p 25

USING THE REFERENCE AREA

To select a microfilm of the part of the census returns you wish to see, you need its reference number (see appendix 4 for a full explanation of reference numbers). To determine this you need to look at one or more reference books, known as finding aids. The books are all clearly labelled by year and contents and are bound in different colours according to the year of the census (see above p 11). They are:

1. Place-name indexes
2. Class lists
3. London street indexes
4. Country street indexes
5. Surname indexes
6. Additional finding aids
    - i) An index to London streets
    - ii) An index to abolished London street names
    - iii) Shipping index
    - iv) List of ecclesiastical parishes
    - v) List of churches and chapels
    - vi) London street directories
    - vii) Maps
    - viii) Population tables
    - ix) Miscellaneous topographical indexes

The census returns, as explained above (p 5), are arranged in numerical order of the superintendent registrar's districts. This presupposes that you know in which order they are numbered so that you can find your way around the country. Once into your registration district you need to know which sub-district contains your place, and so on. Each set of census returns has an index to place names based on the index provided with the printed population tables. This is insufficient, however, when searching large towns, where it is totally impractical to read every frame on the film in the hope of finding the information you seek. Places with a population of over 40,000 have, therefore, been provided with a street index to take you to the correct folios of the enumerator's returns. These street indexes are provided by the PRO. Appendixes 6-10 list all the places covered for each census year.

To search the returns, therefore, you have three options at the outset. If you want to look at a small village or town, consult the place-name index and then the class list (see 1 and 2 below). Alternatively, if you are searching a large town with a population of over 40,000 (then, not now), you need a street index to narrow your search (see 3 and 4 below).

Benjamin Disraeli Independent HO 107/733, book 14 f 45 p 14

If you are looking for an individual, however, especially in 1851, you may find that there is a surname index to your district (see 5 below). The 1881 census is totally indexed, see p 67.

1 PLACE-NAME INDEXES

The indexes of place names include the names of registration districts and of every other smaller division.

The index to places for 1841 gives you a page number to go to in the class list (see 2 below). Place indexes for other years simply give you the name and number of the registration district in which that place occurs and, since the class lists are arranged in numerical order of registration district, it is a quick process to go from the place-name index to the class list in order to obtain the reference you need to identify your reel of film.

PLACE NAME INDEX FOR 1841 CENSUS RETURNS		
PLACE NAME	COUNTY ABBREV.	REF. BOOK PAGE NUMBER
Elmstead	Essex	90
Elmstead	Kent	144
Elmsthorpe	Leics	172
Elmstone	Kent	139
Elmstone Hardwicke	Glos	96,103
Elmstree	Glos	100
Elmton	Derb	52
Elm, Little	Som	303
Elm, North	Som	301
Elsdon	Northumb	249
Elsdon Ward	Northumb	249
Elsecar	Yorks WR	449
Elsenham	Essex	91
Elsey	Lincs	193
Elsfield	Oxon	269
Elsham	Lincs	187
Elsing	Norf	224
Elslack	Yorks WR	440
Elson	Salop	291
Elstead	Surrey	342
Elsted	Sussex	350
Elsthorpe	Lincs	177
Elstob	Durh	82
Elston	Lancs	151
Elston	Notts	264,267
Elston	Wilts	377
Elstow	Beds	2
Elstree	Herts	130
Elstree	Midd	203
Elstronwick	Yorks ER	398
Elstub	Wilts	377
Elswick	Lancs	151
Elswick	Northumb	87
Elsworth	Cambs	17

1841

Place-name indexes, to show not just the registration district number but also whether there is a street index and a surname index available for each particular place, are on the shelves of the reference area. When you look up your place in the place-name index you will discover the number of the registration district in which it can be found. This registration district number is repeated in the street index and surname index columns wherever a place has been so indexed. If these two columns are blank then no street or surname index has been compiled for that place. In this instance you simply proceed to the class

PLACE NAME INDEX FOR 1861 CENSUS RETURNS						
PLACE NAME	COUNTY ABBREV	DISTRICT NAME	DIST NO.	SUB D.No	STREET INDEX	NAME INDEX
Bentley	Hants	Alton	114	2		
Bentley	Staffs	Walsall	380	1		
Bentley	Suff	Samford	221	2		
Bentley	Warw	Atherstone	397	1		
Bentley	Yorks ER	Beverley	518	2		
Bentley	Yorks WR	Doncaster	510	4		
Bentley Pauncefoot	Worcs	Bromsgrove	392	3		
Bentley, Great	Essex	Tendring	203	1		
Bentley, Little	Essex	Tendring	203	5		
Bentley, Lower	Worcs	Bromsgrove	392	3		
Bentley, Upper	Worcs	Bromsgrove	392	3		
Bentworth	Hants	Alton	114	1		
Benwell	Northumb	Newcastle upon Tyne	552	1	552	
Benwick	Cambs	North Witchford	191	1		
Beoley	Worcs	Kings Norton	393	1	393	
Bepton	Sussex	Midhurst	93	3		
Berden	Essex	Bishop Stortford	139	2		
Bere Regis	Dors	Wareham	273	4		
Bere Regis	Dors	Blandford	270	1		
Berechurch	Essex	Colchester	204	1		
Bergholt, East	Suff	Samford	221	1		
Bergholt, West	Essex	Lexdon	205	4		
Berkeley	Glos	Thornbury	332	3		
Berkeswell	Warw	Meriden	396	2		
Berkhampstead	Herts	Berkhampstead	147	1		
Berkhampstead St Mary	Herts	Berkhampstead	147	1		
Berkhampstead, Great	Herts	Berkhampstead	147	1		
Berkhampstead, Little	Herts	Hertford	142	2		

1861

index has been compiled for that place. In this instance you simply proceed to the class

Robert M Ballantyne Literature (Chiefly Juvenile Fiction) RG 11/1357, f 9 p 11

list. A complete listing of surname indexes is supplied in a binder on each set of shelves which shows not only those marked in the place name index but also recent acquisitions.

2 CLASS LISTS

If you find there is no surname or street index for the place you wish to search, consult the place-name index and make a note of the registration district number in the column by the side of your place which is highlighted in yellow. You should next look at the class list for the appropriate year to find how places are grouped together and to ascertain the order in which you can expect to find them on the microfilm. The class list is arranged in numerical order of registration district so you need to discover the correct number before you look at the list.

In 1841 the census returns are grouped by hundreds, and in the northern counties, wapentakes, rather than by registration districts. From the place-name index you will be guided to the **page** of the class list where your place occurs.

Reference		HEREFORDSHIRE		HO 107
HO 107	HUNDRED	PARISH	TOWNSHIP	HAMLET
418	Broxash	Avenbury		
		Bodenham	Bodenham	
			Bowley	
			Bryan-Maund	
			Whitchurch-Maund	
			The Moor	
		Bredenbury		
		Bromyard	Brockhampton	
			(3)Linton	
			Norton	
			Winslow	
		Bockleton(part)*	Hampton-Charles	
		Collington		
		Little Cowarne		
		Much Cowarne		

In all other census years the place-name index will give you a registration district number. The class lists, arranged in numerical order of registration district, will show places grouped together by sub-district within each registration district.

			Llanveynoe	
			Longtown	
			Newton	
		Cusop		
		Cwmyoy(part)*	Bwlch Trewyn	
			Fwthog or Toothog	
			Llancillo	
		St Margaret's		
		Michael-Church-Eskley		
		Rowlstone		
		Walterstone		

HO 107/418 * Rest is in HO 107/1192
HO 107/419 * Rest is in HO 107/1194
HO 107/420 * Rest is in HO 107/742

- 122 -

1841

Each civil parish will include townships and hamlets, not all of which will necessarily be found in the same sub-district or registration district. A cross-referencing system in the footnotes to the class list will tell you where the rest of the parish may be found.

When you discover the exact place you want, the number in the reference column of the list, together with the group and class code in the box at the head of that column, is the full reference you need to identify your film. See appendix 4 for a fuller explanation of the PRO referencing system.

Arthur Chappell Music Publisher HO 107/1475, f 410 p 20

15

Where a return does not survive the class list will show it as 'MISSING'.

Class lists also show you, by means of a bracketed number, the whereabouts of barracks, institutions and shipping. The key to these numbers is to be found in front of each class list and is as follows:

(1) barracks and military quarters
(2) HM ships at home
(3) workhouses (including pauper schools)
(4) hospitals (sick, convalescent, incurable)
(5) lunatic asylums (public and private)
(6) prisons
(7) certified reformatories and industrial schools
(8) merchant vessels
(9) schools

3 LONDON STREET INDEXES

If your search is in the returns for London you will certainly need a street index before you start to look in order to narrow your search. To attempt a search anywhere in London without such specific information is impractical; working through film after film on the off-chance of picking up one particular entry is a forlorn hope. The moment when you blink may be the moment the entry you want appears in the frame.

London is divided into about 36 registration districts, depending on the particular year (see appendix 5). After you have found in which registration district your particular street falls by consulting Book 90 (see 6 (i)), go next to the appropriate index in one of the London street index volumes on the shelves containing the finding aids for your particular census year. These follow the class lists on the shelves and contain the Western and Northern districts, the Central and Eastern districts and the Southern districts of London from Kensington to Greenwich. They do not include West Ham which, although considered part of London now, was in Essex in the nineteenth century.

STREET INDEX TO THE 1861 CENSUS		
CLERKENWELL	THE PIECE NUMBER OF YOUR FILM	TO FIND YOUR PLACE ON THE FILM
Street		Folios
Warner Street, Great, Great Bath Street 1-30	RG9/194	81-81
pt 16	RG9/194	100
Warner Street, Little, Roy Street	RG9/191	78-82
Warren Cottages, Warren Street	RG9/195	100-101
Warren Street, White Conduit Street 1-33	RG9/195	93-105
2B & 3½	RG9/195	100
14	RG9/195	105
Warren Cottages	RG9/195	100-101
Waterloo Place, Clerkenwell Close	RG9/191	12-16
Wellington Place, Wellington Street	RG9/196	23-24
Wellington Street, Rodney Street 1-39	RG9/196	15-23
Pt 5 & 13	RG9/196	36
West Place, Chapel Street 2-7	RG9/195	50-51
Weston Street, Pentonville Road 1-26	RG9/196	135-141
1a & 1b	RG9/196	141
Wharton Street, Bagnigge Wells Road 1-35	RG9/192	66-73
Whisken Street, St John Street Road 36-62	RG9/199	77-90
White Conduit Place, White Conduit Street	RG9/195	82-83
White Conduit Street, Chapel Street	RG9/195	83-87
White Lion Buildings, White Lion Street	RG9/195	28-29
White Lion Street, Islington High Street		
1-pt 45	RG9/195	1-9
Penitentiary	RG9/195	33-34
55-105	RG9/195	33-43
(Part 46 and 47-) Wilderness Row, Go		

1861 LONDON STREET INDEX

Each street index has a title page showing you the sub-district divisions and giving the piece numbers which cover those sub-districts. The index itself lists the streets, buildings, terraces and areas together with house numbers. Each entry is followed by two columns of figures. The first is headed 'To Order Your Film' (or 'To Select Your Film' or 'The Piece Number of Your Film') and provides the reference of the film you require. The second column is headed 'To Find Your Place on the Film' and gives you a folio number, or set of folio numbers, where a particular street will appear on the film. All documents are foliated before being filmed as a security measure to ensure that nothing is omitted from the filming and to provide a reference number when you need to refer to a particular page. These numbers are stamped on the top right-hand corner of every other page of the document, the page without a folio number being identified as the reverse of the preceding page and taking the same folio number.

```
                    1871 CENSUS

                   STREET INDEX


          REGISTRATION DISTRICT 12


                 H O L B O R N


Sub-Districts   1   St. George the Martyr    RG10/369-372
                2   St. Andrew Eastern       RG10/373-375
                3   Saffron Hill             RG10/376-378
                4   St. James Clerkenwell    RG10/379-383
                5   Amwell                   RG10/384-387
                6   Pentonville              RG10/388-391
                7   Goswell Street           RG10/392-395
                8   Old Street               RG10/396-398
                9   City Road                RG10/399-403
               10   Whitecross Street        RG10/404-408
               11   Finsbury                 RG10/409-411
```

You may not necessarily find a street all in one place on the film. The enumerator liked to save his shoe leather, and whilst going up and down a street would also take in side streets where they occurred, before returning to the main street to continue his rounds. You may, therefore, often find more than one sequence of folio numbers beside a street name, and also streets which are continued in other registration districts where boundaries cut across a road. This is explained more fully below in 'Finding Your Place on the Film' (p 31).

THE PIECE NUMBER OF YOUR FILM	TO FIND YOUR PLACE ON THE FILM
	Folios

HM Alexandria Victoria The Queen HO 107/1478, f 645 p 19

In 1841 there is one slight difference in the referencing system. You will need a book number as well as a folio number to identify the whereabouts of your street. The foliation in that year started again at the beginning of each book in the box, so that if you cite an 1841 reference without its book number but using a folio number only, it could mean one of several folios with the same number but in different books. The book number together with the folio number identifies a specific page. The book number can be found on every

Reference:- HO 107 / 659 / 5

frame of the film as part of the reference strip and on the title page of each book (where the foliation begins at 1). There it looks like a fraction, the upper number being the piece number and the lower the number of the book.

4 COUNTRY STREET INDEXES

The country street indexes are much the same as the indexes to London registration districts. Places with a population of over 40,000 in the nineteenth century were street indexed. For a list of indexes available see appendixes 6-10. Most have a separate list of public houses, institutions and shipping at the back and some years have some items grouped together under a heading such as Schools, Caravans (this heading includes any travellers even if they are sleeping in a tent). Individually named buildings, terraces and groups of cottages are included, and each index has a title page showing the name of the registration district and its division into sub-districts. Country street indexes do not, however, show house numbers except for larger towns in 1881.

Hamlets included in any township are mentioned as entries in the index itself and not usually on the title page. Over the years other places with a population of less than 40,000 have acquired a street index, or a partial street index where not all of the registration district has been covered. These are not part of the normal run of indexes and will be found in a single volume, covering the years 1841 to 1871, on the officer's desk. They are listed in appendix 10.

Charles Landseer Historical Painter RG 9/56, f 124 p 36

STREET INDEX TO THE 1861 CENSUS CROYDON Street	TO ORDER YOUR FILM	TO FIND YOUR PLACE ON THE FILM Folios
Croydon Lodge, St James Road	RG9/450	31
Croydon Road	RG9/451	118–121
Crystal Palace Lodge	RG9/451	142
Crystal Palace Road, Norwood	RG9/450	78–79
Crystal Terrace	RG9/451	7–10
Dagnall Park	RG9/450	166–168
Dale House, Beaulah Hill	RG9/451	42
Dalletts Cottages, Merton Rush	RG9/453	89–90
Daltons Court, Church Street	RG9/449	71–72
Daniels Cottages, Whitehorse Road	RG9/450	48–49
Dartmill Cottage, New Town		
Deerfield, Beaulah Hill		

Country Street Index

5 SURNAME INDEXES

The PRO does not itself compile surname indexes. There are, however, numerous surname indexes produced by family history societies and published in booklet form, although many are now produced on microfiche instead. For the whereabouts of microfiche readers see the plan of the search room on page vi. Most societies begin with the 1851 census but many have progressed to the other years. The Genealogical Society of Utah and the Federation of Family History Societies indexed jointly the whole of the 1881 census.

Many of these surname indexes are available in the Census Room and more are added each week. If you wish to discover if a place has a surname index, make a note of the registration district number (there is a complete list of registration district names and numbers in appendix 5). Next, go to the drawers where the surname indexes are housed (see plan on page vi); you will find the indexes available arranged in numerical order of registration district in colour-coded envelopes. If no envelope is there for your registration district in the year you wish to search this means that as yet none has been donated. Many surname indexes are now produced on fiche and the envelope will then direct you to the rack in the microfilm area. If a name you want is listed it should also show the reference of the film you need and a folio number which will help you to find your place on the film. See pp 31-42 for an explanation of how to locate places by the use of folio numbers.

John Sanger 'Equestrian Troupe' Circus Proprietor RG 9/2943, f 114 p 6

6 ADDITIONAL FINDING AIDS

6 (i) An index to London streets (Book 90)

When looking up an address in any of the London censuses it is essential to be sure of its registration district. In some census years there are as many as thirty-six registration districts in central London, and you can waste many hours seeking a street in the wrong district unless you do some homework first. It is not enough to consult a map, for it will not tell you the boundaries of a registration district in relation to the street names, and knowing that a street is in Marylebone today does not necessarily mean that it fell within the boundaries of the Marylebone registration district. It may have been borderline and, in census terms, it may have fallen within St Pancras or Hampstead. There is one sure way of finding out.

In 1887 the Metropolitan Board of Works published *Names of Streets and Places within the Metropolitan Area*. This is an instantly forgettable title so the book is referred to as 'Book 90', from its reading room shelf number. It provides a complete list of London streets, terraces, buildings, roads, etc (except for those which changed their name or were abolished before 1855), with the name of the nearest main road in a central column and the name of the parish in which they lie in the right-hand column. The parishes named in the right-hand column are in most cases the same as the names of the appropriate London registration district but occasionally the name of the sub-district. In this case a quick check in the book giving London parishes and localities (see 6(ix)2) will identify the covering

Name.	Postal District.	Locality.	Parish.	Year.
Wharves (The)	S.E.	River-side	East Greenwich	
Wharves .The)	W.	Uxbridge-road	Hammersmith	
Wharncliffe-street	E.	Bonner-street	Bethnal-green	1860
Wharton-place	E.	School-house-lane	Ratcliff	
Wharton-road	W.	Sinclair-gardens	Hammersmith	
Wharton-street	E.C.	King's-cross-road	Clerkenwell	
Whateley-road	S.E.	Kent-house-road	Beckenham	
Whateley-road	S.E.	Lordship-lane	Camberwell	
Whatman-road	S.E.	Brockley-road	Lewisham	1867
Wheathill-road	S.E.	Croydon-road	Ponge	1867
Wheatley's-cottages	S.E.	Ravensbourne-street	Greenwich	
Wheatsheaf alley	S.W.	Bishop's-road	Fulham	
Wheatsheaf-lane	S.W.	South Lambeth-road	Lambeth	
Wheatsheaf lane	S.W.	Upper Tooting	Streatham	
Wheatsheaf-whf.-alley	E.C.	Upper Thames-street	City	

Book 90

registration district for the given sub-district. Then you can proceed confidently to the correct street index for the year you want by consulting the place-name index, obtaining from it the registration district number, and going to the appropriate street index volume.

John Bird Sumner Archbishop of Canterbury HO 107/1571, f 291 p 4

6 (ii) An index to abolished London street names (Books 91 and 92)

Sometimes London streets cannot be found in street indexes even though a birth, marriage or death certificate of a similar date clearly states the address. This is because street names changed, renumbering took place, or new streets were built. When an enumerator collected his information it was quite possible that people still referred to their address by a recently discontinued name, or that a renumbering of a street obscured the fact that, for example, 86 King's Road was once 2 Victoria Cottages. The cottages may still be there with their name on the brickwork, but each of the individual cottages has acquired a number that is part of the road it is on, in place of the number of its particular position in the terrace or group of cottages. Much renumbering of London streets in this way took place in the 1850s and 1860s.

The way round this problem is to look in 'Books 91 and 92' which rejoice in the title *London County Council List of Streets and Places Within the Administrative County of London shewing Localities, Postal Districts, Parishes, Metropolitan Boroughs, Electoral*

Name of Street or Place.	Locality.	Postal District.	Parish.	Metropolitan Borough, or City.	County Electoral and Parliamentary Division.	Ordnance sheet 5 ft. to 1 mile.	Reference to Municipal Map.	Name approved.	Alterations. (1856–1928)		
									Date of Order.	No. of Plan.	Names abolished. / Numbers assigned.
Wet—Whi					550						
Wetherell road	Victoria park road	E.9	Hackney	Hackney	S. Hackney	vii.-29	35–12	1868	30.v.70 2346	Providence row Louisa cottages Albert terrace	1–55 (cons.)
Wexford road	Nightingale lane	S.W.2	Battersea	Battersea	S. Battersea	x.-80 90;	17–37	1894			
Weybourne street	Garratt lane to Steerforth st.	S.W.18	Wandsworth	Wandsworth	Cen. Wandsworth	x.-09	13–40	1913			
Weybridge street	Culvert road	S.W.11	Battersea	Battersea	N. Battersea	xi.-31	18–30	1863	13.ii.12	Carpenter street	
†Weymouth dwellings	Sayer street	S.E.17	Newington	Southwark	S.E. Southwark	vii.-95	29–24				
Weymouth court	Sayer street	S.E.17	Newington	Southwark	S.E. Southwrk.	vii.-95	29–24				
†Weymouth court	Weymouth street	W.1	St. Marylebone	St. Marylebone	St. Marylebone	vii.-52	21–17		1.iii.89 4196	.. ..	1–45 (cons)
Weymouth mews	Weymouth street	W.1	St. Marylebone	St. Marylebone	St. Marylebone	vii.-52	29–17				
Weymouth mews	Weymouth terr.	E.2	Shoreditch	Shoreditch	Shoreditch	vii.-37	33–14		3.iii.76 1756	Upper Weymouth street	1–71; 2–6
Weymouth street	Gt. Portland st. to High street, Marylebone	W.1	St. Marylebone	St. Marylebone	St. Marylebone	vii.-51 52	23–17				
Weymouth terrace	Hackney road	E.2	Shoreditch	Shoreditch	Shoreditch	vii.-27 37	33–13		16.xi.06 508	White's cotts. Prospect terrace Albion place Elizabeth cotts.	1–127 2–142
Whalebone court	Moorgate bldgs.	E.C.2	City of London	City of London	City of London	vii.-66	30–18				
Whalebone passage	Tokenhouse yard	E.C.2	City of London	City of London	City of London	vii.-66	30–18				
Wharf road	Pritchard's road	E.2	Bethnal green	Bethnal green	N.E. Beth. grn.	vii.-28	35–13		9.xii.88 4126	.. ..	1–25; 2–2
Wharf road	Latimer road	W.10	Hammersmith	Hammersmith	N. Hammersmith	vi.-60	7–19		7.xii.53 3309	Eastbourne terr. Wharf terrace	1–43; 2–6
Wharf road	Uxbridge road	W.12	Hammersmith	Hammersmith	N. Hammersmith	vi.-70	8–21				
Wharf road	Ferry street, Cubitt Town	E.14	Poplar Borough	Poplar	S. Poplar	xii.- 2 11 12	44–26				
Wharf road	City road	N.1	Shoreditch and Finsbury	Shoreditch Nos. 1–31 Finsbury Nos. 22–35	Shoreditch 1–21 (cons.) Finsbury 22–35 (cons.)	vii.-35	29–14				
Wharf road	Frogmore	S.W.18	Wandsworth Borough	Wandsworth	Putney	x.-58	12–34		21.v.89 4227	Haydon's cotts.	1–43 (cons)
Wharfdale road	Caledonian road	N.1	Islington	Islington	W. Islington	vii.-33 34	25–13		24.vii.68 789	Wharf road Gordon terrace Albert place Albert terrace St. Stephen's ter. Haverford terr.	1–69; 2–2
Wharfedale street	Coleherne road	S.W.10	Kensington	Kensington	S. Kensington	x.- 8	12–26				
†Wharncliffe gardens	Grove road, St. John's Wood road and Cunningham pl.	N.W.8	St. Marylebone	St. Marylebone	St. Marylebone	vi.-49 56	16–15				
Wharncliffe street	Hartley street	E.2	Bethnal green	Bethnal green	N.E. Bethnal green	vii.-38 39	37–14	1860	6.xii.85 3585	.. ..	1–11; 2–2
Wharton street	King's Cross road	W.C.1	Finsbury	Finsbury	Finsbury	vii.-34 44	25–15				
Whateley road	Lordship lane	S.E.22	Camberwell	Camberwell	Dulwich	xi.-67	33–35		3.xii.86 3797 31.i.05 6604	Whateley terr.	1–55; 2–2
Whatman road	Brockley rise	S.E.23	Lewisham	Lewisham	W. Lewisham	xi.-80	32–37	(1867)	15.xii.03 27.x.22 733		
†Wheatlands road	Tooting Bec road	S.W.17	Wandsworth Borough	Wandsworth	Balham and Balham	xv.- 1	15–41	1906		Book 92	

Divisions, Ordnance and Municipal Map References Together with the Alterations in Street Nomenclature and Numbering since 1856. The Public Record Office has the

Joseph Tussaud Artist RG 10/164, f 13 p 20

revised edition, compiled by the Superintendent Architect of the Council and published in 1912. It is in two volumes: 'Book 91' covering A to Lily and 'Book 92' covering Limasol to Z. You will see in many cases a 'date of order' in a column after the street name; this means that at that date an order went through for some adjustment in the street name. Some time after this date the change would have been put into effect. These volumes, however, like Book 90, do not include the names of streets abolished or changed before 1855.

6 (iii) Shipping index (Book 95)

Shipping on rivers and within territorial waters was included in the census returns at the end of the districts where the ships lay but it was not until 1861 that shipping on the high seas and in foreign ports was enumerated and then only some of it. Returns from such ships are found in the special shipping schedules at the end of the returns from 1861 onwards. There is an index to the names of ships compiled from these schedules and also a set of microfiche which indexes all the people on board for 1861 only.

6 (iv) List of ecclesiastical parishes (Book 94)

It frequently happens that a particular place required by a searcher is an ecclesiastical district and cannot be found in the list of places because the census was enumerated in civil parishes. Obviously the ecclesiastical district exists, but it is necessary to determine in which civil parish it rests. To do this consult the list of parishes. This is a four volume book, bound in black, that will tell you in most instances the name of the ecclesiastical parish in the left-hand column followed by the civil parish in the next column. There is also a column giving the poor law union, which is the same as the registration district. Armed with the name of the registration district and appropriate civil parish you can discover the reference by the normal procedure.

Once you have the film on the machine and you have turned on to the civil parish indicated you will see, if the enumerator has done his job correctly, that there is a box at the top of the page labelled 'ecclesiastical district' which should be completed and therefore contain the place name you originally sought. If it is not, turn back to the title page of that enumeration district where you may find mention of the ecclesiastical district and be reassured that it has been enumerated in that part of the film.

James Burn Editor of the ABC Railway Guide RG 10/1322, f 62 p 12

13.

Name of Ship	Whereabouts	Reference RG 9
BACCHUS	Bristol	4498
BACCHUS	Llanelly	4530
BADGER	North Sea	4450
BALBIC	Liverpool	4507
BALCLUTHA	A.S.	4438
BALFOUR	Dudgeon Light	4463
BALLARRAT	At Sea	4458
BALLARAT	Dieppe	4459
BALLINASLOE	Birkenhead	450
BALLINDALLACH	At Sea	4462

Book 95

	Parish or Place.	United with or included in	Division.	County.	Description.	Tax Survey.	Poor Law Union.	Collector of I. R.
1	Essington	Essington, &c.	Cuttlestone	Stafford	Tp.	STAFFORD	Cannock	Wolverhampton.
2	Estacott	(Northoe P.)	Braunton	Devon	Ham.	BARNSTAPLE	Barnstaple	Exeter.
3	Eston		Langbaurgh East	Yorks	Tp.	STOCKTON	Middlesbrough	Sunderland.
4	Estyn	Caergwrley, &c.	Mold	Flint	Ham.	CHESTER	Hawarden	Chester.
5	Estynallon	Bodlith, &c.	Cynlleth and Mochnant.	Denbigh	Tp.	WREXHAM	Oswestry Incorporation.	Chester.
6	Etal	(Ford P.)	Glendale	Northumb.	—	ALNWICK	Glendale	Newcastle.
7	Etchells	Northenden, &c.	Stockport	Cheshire	L.T.P.	STOCKPORT	Altrincham and Stockport.	Manchester.
8	Etchells in Northern	Etchells in Northern, &c.	Stockport	Cheshire	Par.	STOCKPORT	-	Stockport.
9	Etchilhampton	Etchilhampton, &c.	Devizes	Wilts	L.T.P.	CHIPPENHAM	Devizes	Bath.
10	Etchingham		Hastings Rape (Battle).	Sussex	Par.	HASTINGS	Ticehurst	Canterbury.
11	Etherley *Etherdwick*	(Escomb Tp.)	Darlington Ward	Durham *Yorks*	Ham.	DARLINGTON	Auckland	Sunderland.
12	Ethy	St. Winnow Lostwithiel.	-	Cornwall	—	BODMIN	-	Plymouth.
13	Ethirick	(St. Dominick P.)	East Middle	Cornwall	Ham.	LAUNCESTON	Liskeard	Plymouth.
14	Eton	-	Stoke	Bucks	Par. & L.B.	WINDSOR	Eton	Reading.
15	Etton	-	Peterborough	Northampton	Par.	PETERBOROUGH	Peterborough	Lincoln.
16	Etruria	(Shelton P.)	Pirehill North	Stafford	—	STOKE-ON-TRENT	Stoke-on-Trent	Derby.
17	Etterby	Brunstock, &c.	Eskdale Ward	Cumberland	L.T.P.	CARLISLE	Carlisle	Carlisle.
18	Ettiley Heath	(Sandbach P.)	Northwich	Cheshire	Ham.	CREWE	Congle	
19	Ettingshall	(Bilston P.)	Seisdon	Stafford	Ham.	WOLVERHAMPTON	Wolve	

ESSI

188

Book 94

The Duchess of Orleans HO 107/1604, f 122 p 37

6 (v) List of churches and chapels wherein marriages are solemnised according to the rites of the established church 1871 (Book 96)

As its rather lengthy title suggests, this volume is a list of churches and chapels, grouped alphabetically by the name of the registration district into which they fall. Its value is that, having located a family in the census returns, a searcher may need to continue the hunt for families in parish registers. After consulting 'Book 96' you will know which parish or nonconformist registers to consult. This list is part of an annual series from which the one for 1871 has been selected for use in the Census Room. You may find when seeking parish records in the area in an earlier period that not all the churches listed in 1871 will be in existence. The ecclesiastical census of 1851 (HO 129 held at the Public Record Office, Kew) surveys places of worship at that date.

		PLACES OF PUBLIC WORSHIP Registered for Solemnization of Marriages under the Provisions of the Acts of 6 & 7 Wm. IV. c. 85., and 1 Victoria, c. 22.		
SUPERINTENDENT REGISTRAR'S DISTRICT, and COUNTY.	CHURCHES AND CHAPELS wherein Marriages are solemnised according to the Rites of the Established Church.	Name.	Where situated.	Religious Denomination.
WESTHAMP-NETT. *Sussex.* (82.) II.*	1. Birdham. 1. Earnley. 1. Itchenor, West. 1. Selsey. 1. Sidlesham. 1. Wittering, East. 1. ———— West. 2. Appledram. 2. Donnington. 2. Fishbourne, New. 2. Hunstan. 2. Merston. 2. Mundham, North. 2. Pagham. 2. Rumboldswyke. 3. Bersted. 3. Bignor. 3. Barnham. 4. Binstead. 4. Eastergate. 4. Felpham. 4. Madehurst. 4. Middleton. 4. Slindon. 4. Walberton. 4. Yapton. 5. Aldingbourne. 5. Boxgrove. 5. Eartham. 5. Lavant, East. 5. Oving. 5. Tangmore. 5. Westhampnett. 6. Dean, East. 6. Lavant, Mid. 6. Singleton. 6. Stoke, West. 6. Upwaltham.	St. Richard's Church Hanover Chapel -	Slindon - Bognor -	Roman Catholics. Independents.
WESTMINSTER. *Middlesex.* (4.) I.*	1. Westminster, St. James. 2. ———— St. Thomas, Regent-street. 3. ———— St. Luke. 3. ———— St. Peter, Great Windmill Street. 4. St. Anne, within the Liberty of Westminster. 5. St. Mary, Soho.	Craven Chapel - Bavarian Chapel - St. James's Scotch Church. St. Patrick's Chapel Independent Chapel Soho Chapel - - Salem Chapel - Nassau-street Chapel	Marshall-st., Golden-sq. Warwick-street, Regent-street. Swallow-street, Piccadilly. Sutton-street, Soho-square. Little Chapel-street, Soho. Oxford-street Meard's-court Nassau-st., Soho	Independents. Roman Catholics. EstablishedCh. of Scotland. Roman Catholics. Independents. Particular Baptists. Particular Baptists. Welsh Calv. Methodists.
WEST WARD - *Westmorland.* (575.) X.b	1. Bolton. 1. Cliburn. 1. Crosby Ravensworth. 1. Mardale. 1. Morland. 1. Shap. 2. Askham. 2. Bampton. 2. Barton. 2. Brougham Rectory. 2. ———— Chapel. 2. Clifton. 2. Lowther. 2. Martindale. 2. Patterdale.			

Book 96

Do not forget that if ancestors do not seem to appear in appropriate parish registers, they may have been nonconformist. Many researchers disregard non-conformist records, many of which are held in the Public Record Office in the record classes RG 4 to RG 8, because they assume that the family have always been Anglicans. Nonconformity was very popular in the nineteenth century especially amongst some classes of people such as industrial workers, artisans and tradesmen, and your ancestors may have tried what was the current trend. The nonconformist registers in the record class RG 4 are indexed on the International Genealogical Index, a copy of which is available in the Census Room (see D Shorney, *Sources for the History of Non-Conformity* Public Record Office Readers' Guide, Number 13).

William T Mitford Magistrate Deputy Lieutenant RG 11/140, f 79 pp 13-14

6 (vi) London street directories

The London street directories are not only useful for tracing individuals from their known trades or professions, but can also help when you are faced with multiple entries for a street in a street index. Where there are several references in a street index, and no indication as to which one contains the house number you want, turn to the street directory. Look up your street, find your house number and note the names of the two side streets (written in italics) nearest to your house number, and then go back to the street index. Look up the references to the side streets and select similar references from the selection given for your long street. Remember that some streets may run on into another registration district.

The Public Record Office makes available the street directories for the year following a census year in order to allow for the compilation and printing of information gathered in the actual census year. Even so, as is often the case today, these may have errors at the time of going to press; so, if persons are not listed in the directory under the address you expect, you may still find them there on the film.

6 (vii) Maps

Instinctively one turns to a map when difficulties are encountered in locating a place, either while searching in the indexes or after finding a birthplace on the microfilms. Sometimes it is much quicker to turn to a gazetteer or one of the additional finding aids before going to a map because most maps do not relate to census divisions.

The Public Record Office makes available a book of parish maps, known as the Phillimore Atlas, arranged by county, published by the Institute of Heraldic and Genealogical Studies at Canterbury and available for purchase from them, from the Public Record Office shop and from the Society of Genealogists. This is useful when a parish does not include the family you are looking for and you need to cast your net wider and search the surrounding parishes.

There are also two sets of maps in the Public Record Office at Kew which give the boundaries of the registration districts, sub-districts and the civil parishes. One set, correct for the years 1851 to 1861, is not complete, as some of the maps do not survive. The other is a complete set for 1891 (for both sets see the class list for RG 18). Note your registration district number when using the 1891 set since that is the way the maps are arranged within the counties.

These maps are most useful when an individual large house or a tiny hamlet cannot be found in street indexes or other finding aids. Once the place is located on the map the parish containing it can be determined by noting the place name which has a pink line through it within the thin red boundary line. Then note the sub-district by observing the pink boundaries within which the place falls, and the large pink spot on the place which gives its name to the sub-district. Finally, note the green boundary lines and the green spot on the place which is the name of the registration district, and return to the lists and indexes for the year you wish to research.

Copies of these maps may be obtained from the microfilm version; ask at the reading room officer's desk in the Census Room. The films are not as clear as the originals because the colour has not been reproduced and the fine detail of the map is difficult to read on film. Colour copies of the RG 18 maps will be available for consultation by early 1998.

Charles Mark (Karl Marx) Dr (philosophical author) HO 107/1510, f 260 p 11

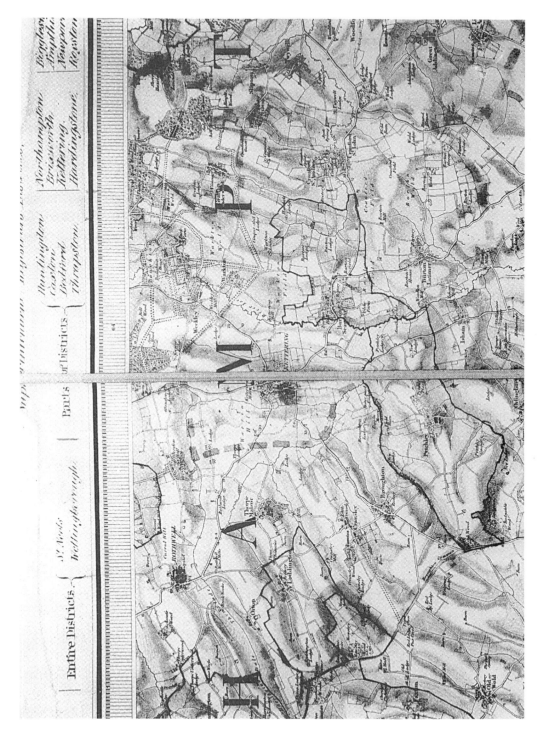

Part of a map showing Kettering and the surrounding census districts.   RG 18/52

The Greater London Record Office has published a list of known eighteenth-century maps of London; the Guildhall Library and the Bishopsgate Institute also have useful map collections. An *A-Z of Georgian London* and an *A-Z of Victorian London* have been published by the London Topographical Society; equally valuable is the series of Victorian Ordnance Survey Maps published by Godfrey.

The appropriate local record office or local history or family history societies may be able to help if you are in difficulties with any particular place. They will have local knowledge not available in the Census Room.

For the London area the Society of Genealogists has published a map showing London registration district boundaries in relation to borough boundaries and the boundaries of the local family history societies. This is available at the PRO shop and at the Society.

6 (viii) Population tables

Once the census returns had been thoroughly checked by the enumerators and their supervisors, the information collected was published as a set of Parliamentary Papers; copies of these for all census years may be seen at the officer's desk. The tables, like the class lists, are arranged in numerical order of registration district and give the breakdown of an area into registration districts, sub-districts and townships. They also give the acreage of each township. Then follows a count of houses and population for each place, both for the year being enumerated and for the previous census year. The footnotes give useful additional information; eg why a local population varied markedly from the previous census, or where institutions (as defined on p 37), or lists of railway navvies, may be

610 YORKSHIRE—35. WEST RIDING.—Area ; Houses and Inhabitants, 1851 an				HOUSES.				
SUPERINTENDENT REGISTRAR'S DISTRICT.		Area in Statute Acres.	1851.				186	
Sub-district.	Parish, Township, or Place.		Inha-bited.	Un-inha-bited.	Build-ing.	Inha-bited.	Un-inha-bited	
495. TODMORDEN.								
1. Hebden Bridge	*Halifax, part of Parish—* Wadsworth - - Township	10080	957	166	–	923	15¢	
	Erringden - - Township	2980	353	47	1	371	44	
	Heptonstall - - *Township	6320	882	127	2	790	17¢	
	Stansfield, *part of* * - * Township [viz., the Lower Third Division.]	} 5920-	353	95	3	320	9¢	
2. Todmorden -	*Halifax, part of Parish—* Stansfield, *part of* * - Township [viz., the Middle Third and Upper Third Division.]		1132	102	11	1361	6¢	
	Langfield - - Township	2620	752	41	55	890	31	
	Rochdale, part of Parish— Todmorden and Walsden }Townp. (Lancashire) - - }	–	1481	114	31	1790	6¢	
496. SADDLEWORTH.								
1. Delph¹ᵇ - -	Saddleworth, *part of* † - Township (*part of Rochdale Parish*²)	} 18280	1819	230	10	2048	18¢	
2. Upper Mill ¹ᵇ -	Saddleworth, *part of* (W) † Township (*part of Rochdale Parish*³)		1548	105	18	1770	11¢	
497. HUDDERSFIELD.								
1. Slaithwaite -	*Huddersfield, part of Parish—* Slaithwaite - - Township²	3320	553	29	7	875	1:	
	Marsden { in *Huddersfield Parish*ᶜ -	2050	103	9	6	138	1¢	
	Tnp.‡ ⁴ { in *Almondbury Parish* §ᵉ -	5061	407	50	4	428	2:	
	Almondbury, part of Parish—§ * Lingards - - - Township	500	159	4	–	149		
	Linthwaite, *part of* ‖ - ᶠ Township	809	264	13	–	309	1¢	
2. Meltham - -	*Almondbury, part of Parish—*§ * South Crosland - - Township	1560	536	36	2	582	3¢	
	Meltham - - - Township	4525	684	42	20	795	7¢	
3. Honley -	*Almondbury, part of Parish—*§ * Honley (W) - - *Township	2790	1077	35	17	987	18¢	
	Netherthong - - Township	850	228	13	5	223	3¢	

John W Millais Proprietor of Houses HO 107/1509, f 75 p 14

found. Copies of these tables are kept in the Census Room in case clarification is required of places falling within a registration district or information is needed about the fluctuation of population in an area. A list of these publications will be found in the bibliography (appendix 11).

6(ix) Miscellaneous topographical indexes

As indexing of census returns has progressed over the years much useful information has been collected to assist in identifying the whereabouts of places and particular addresses, especially in London.

There are six indexes available at the officer's desk which may help to identify places which do not occur in the place-name indexes, or which may be useful when searching for places in London.

1. County variations and divided parishes
2. Parishes and localities
3. Divided streets
4. Renumbered streets
5. Missing streets
6. Postal districts

Identifying a particular part of London can be quite complex as some streets appear in more than one index. Ask the reading room officer to help you if you need to use these volumes.

FROM REFERENCE TO MICROFILM

Once you have discovered your reference then go and find your seat. Beyond the reference area you will find the microfilm readers and film cabinets (see page vi for a plan

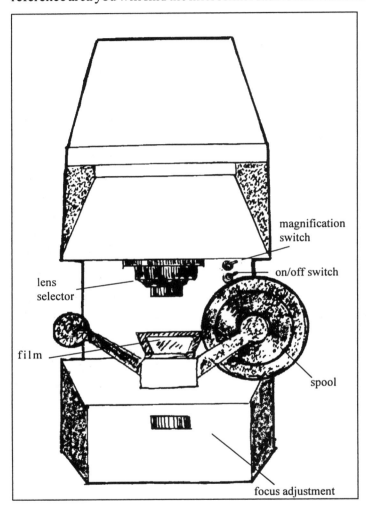

of the reading rooms). Your seat number is on the edge of the table holding the microfilm reader and will be repeated on the black 'dummy' box located on a ledge to the right of each reader. Take this black box with you to the microfilm cabinets that you will find at the entrance to the area containing the microfilm reader area. The films are in numerical sequence of reference number and you will see that the cabinet drawers are clearly labelled with the first and last references held within them. When you open the drawer, you will find there is a locking mechanism which allows only one drawer in a stack to be opened at any one time. You will see the reference numbers marked on the side of the

film boxes; select the one you need and replace it with the black box giving your seat number. When you return the film retrieve the black box. Please be sure to put your film back in the right drawer when you have finished with it. If the film cabinets are locked at the end of the day before you finish with a film after that time you cannot put it away. Just leave it on top of the cabinet in which it belongs and the staff will put it away and retrieve your dummy box later.

Alfred Tennyson Poet Laureate HO 107/1698, f 493 p 26

MICROFILM READERS

To thread your reel of film on to the microfilm reader you need to attach the reel to the spindle on the left-hand side of the machine. Next thread the film from the bottom of

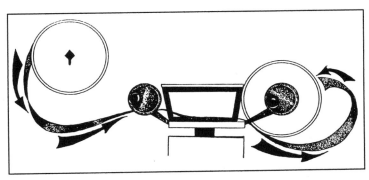

the reel to the right, under the gate and on to the empty spool on the right-hand spindle. Do not thread the film over the top of the right-hand reel but carry on moving the film to the right under the empty spool and bring it up on the outside of the spool and over the top in an anti-clockwise direction. Engage the end into the slot in the centre of the spool, as shown in the diagram. When going through the film quickly in order to reach a particular piece number, open the gate of the microfilm reader; there is then less wear and tear on the film. Once you are in the right piece number, close the gate and start looking at the detail.

You will find two lens settings directly above the gate which are changed by turning the bevelled wheel to the right or left as required. The on/off switch is to the right of the machine, and the focus button is in the front of the base. Microfilm readers must be switched off when not in use to avoid over-heating and damage to the film, which is liable to happen within even a few minutes. There are instructions at the reading room officer's desk, and at intervals around the search room, which explain how to load and operate a microfilm reader.

If the plastic spool is worn in the middle so that it will not run smoothly when turning the handle, ask a reading room officer to change it for you.

FINDING YOUR PLACE ON THE FILM

Once you have the film correctly threaded onto the machine you can start your search. Without having seen the original enumerators' books it must be difficult to understand the system you find. Remember that the enumerators handed out schedules to householders in the week preceding census night and collected them up on the Monday morning immediately after the Sunday night - it was always a Sunday - of the census (see appendix 1 for the dates of the 1841 to 1891 censuses). The enumerator then had to enter

Edwin Landseer Artist HO 107/678, book 4 f 8 p 9

the information from these schedules into a book and provide a description of his district on the title page. Some went further and provided maps or comments about the people they met. Most listed either the streets that were included in their enumeration district or the streets **surrounding** their area (in other words streets which do not appear in the following enumeration district but which define the area to be covered because they surround it). In 1891 the style of these title pages was altered to help clarify the parts of administrative divisions occurring in each enumeration district (see p 54). Even then it is difficult to discover exactly where some smaller places occur as the enumerators, having completed these new title pages, did not always repeat the place names in the box headings at the top of each page (see also p 65). The enumerator also had to complete a summary page of the totals of males and females and buildings he had encountered (see p 34).

Each of these books, therefore, has a title page, a page of instructions and a printed example of a completed form, a page of tables for the enumerator to complete, an abstract of totals and a page declaring that the information is correct (see pp 33-36). It is only after all this that the information about individuals begins.

The enumerators' books are bound into folders, about five or six at a time depending on their size. When these folders were filmed, they were first foliated for security, as a check that all had been included on the microfilm and to provide a precise reference when needing to identify a page. This means that the top right-hand corner of every other page is stamped with a sequence of numbers that begins and ends within that one folder, except in 1841 and 1851 when each box of folders was

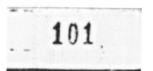

foliated throughout. Consequently when you obtain a reference for 1841 or 1851 it will cover more than a similar reference for other census years. You will find that your piece number (the third element of your reference, see appendix 4) may cover more than one film, whereas for 1861-1891 you may get several piece numbers to a single film. So when you put your film onto the machine, depending on which year you are looking at, you need to make sure that you are in the right part of the film.

Each frame on the film has a strip down one side, or along the bottom, with the reference number on it. Since you will be selecting either a film with several different references, or a film that is only part of one reference, you need to check these strips until you have found the right reference for your place. Once you are into that part of the film you can narrow your search further.

William Hamley   Toy Dealer   RG 9/170, f 30 p 17

58

Superintendent Registrar's District _____

Registrar's Sub-District _____

Enumeration District, No. 4 _____

Name of Enumerator, Mr. *Henry Dyer*

DESCRIPTION OF ENUMERATION DISTRICT.

[This description is to be written in by the Enumerator from the Copy supplied to him by the Registrar. Any explanatory notes or observations calculated to make the description clearer or more complete, may be added by the Enumerator].

From and including Lower Great Percy Street both sides, also
east side of Baynes or Wells Row, including Police Court
and Police Station; also King's Terrace North, taking Wharton
Street both sides.

Comprising ———

No. 1 to 25 A and 32 to 39 Great Percy Street No 27 and
28 Baynes or Wells Row Police Court and Police Station
No 1 to 8 King's Terrace North and No 1 to 52 Wharton Street and
Percy Grove.

Title page to an 1861 enumeration district.   RG 9/192, f 58 p (i)

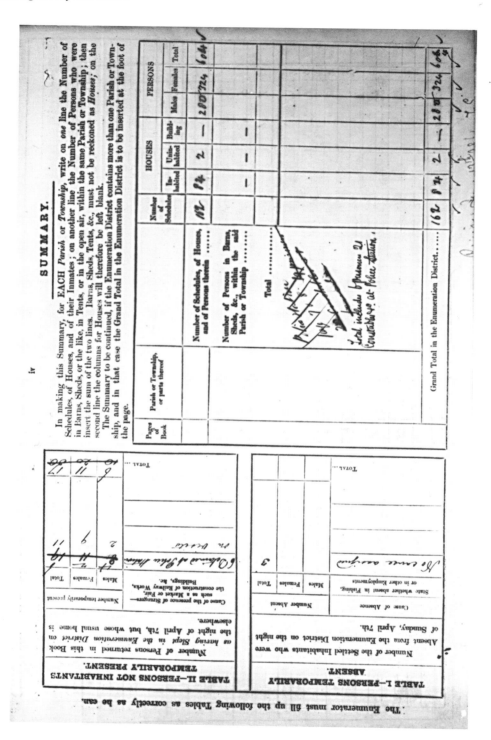

Summary page of an enumerator's book.   RG 9/192, f 59 p (iv)

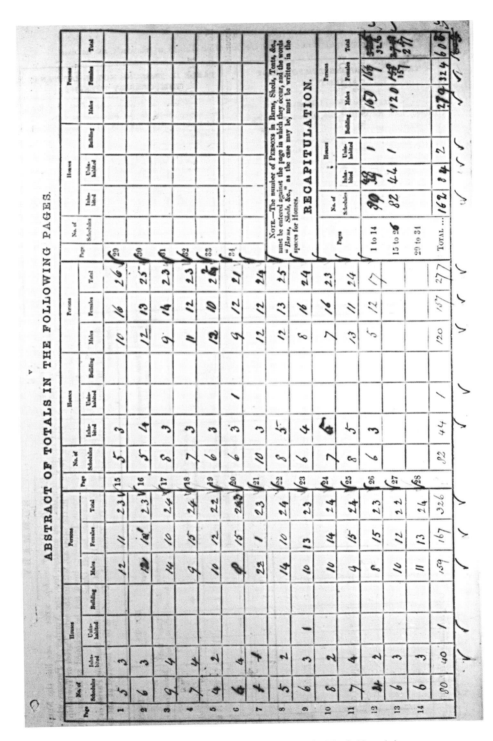

Abstract of totals from an enumerator's book.   RG 9/192, f 60 p (v)

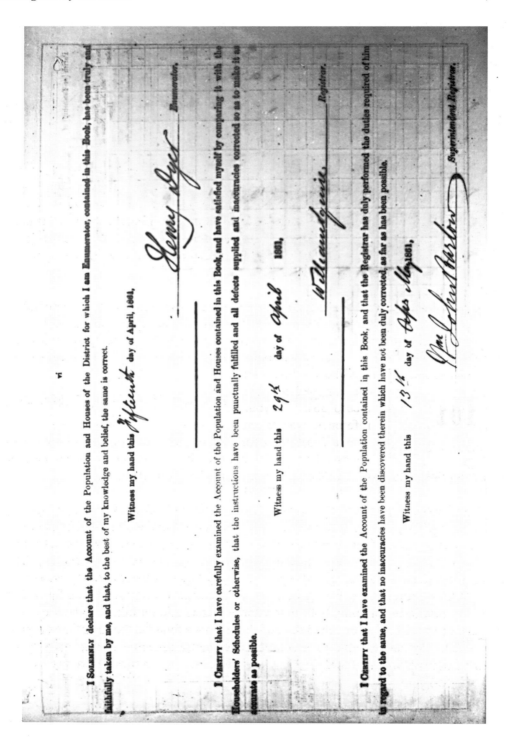

Statement of accuracy from an enumerator's book.   RG 9/192, f 60 p (vi)

58

Superintendent Registrar's District *Clerkenwell*   Enumeration District, No. *4*

Registrar's Sub-District *Amwell*   Name of Enumerator, Mr. *Henry Dyer*

DESCRIPTION OF ENUMERATION DISTRICT.

[This description is to be written in by the Enumerator from the Copy supplied to him by the Registrar. Any explanatory notes or observations calculated to make the description clearer or more complete, may be added by the Enumerator].

From and including Lower Great Percy Street, both sides, along east side of Bagnigge Wells Road, including Police Court.

If you picked up a reference from the class list then you need to start looking at the title pages of the books which occur at regular intervals - remember there are five or six of these in each piece number - or at the boxed headings on each page for your place. Bearing in mind that each civil parish can contain numerous hamlets, tithings or townships, you need to search for your particular one before applying yourself to the information on the page.

Page 20]

Parish [or Township] of *St James Clerkenwell*

Road. Street. &c.

If you have found your reference from a street index for 1841-1871 or a surname index, you will be seeking a particular folio number. Remember that a folio number covers two pages so do not just look at the page on which the folio number is stamped but also on the following page which, although without a stamped number, is the reverse of the page with the stamped number (see p 56). If your reference was taken

101

Enumeration District, No. 4

from a street index for 1881 or 1891 you will be looking for an enumeration district number which is written by the enumerator on the top right-hand corner of the title pages of the books on the film.

There are two exceptions to the above. Institutions such as workhouses, hospitals, asylums or military barracks, providing they contained at least two hundred inhabitants, were given the status of enumeration districts in their own right and are found at the end of each district on special forms which have no address column (see pp 38 and 39). The information given is sometimes not very useful as birthplaces are frequently not known ('N.K.'), but other records covering these particular categories may yield the information required. Similarly, shipping both in territorial waters and on inland waterways was recorded on special shipping schedules and these too are found at the end of the districts (see p 22). For an example of a completed shipping schedule see pp 40 and 41. Unfortunately not many of these shipping schedules survive in the 1891 returns.

Joseph Cash Mnf of Silk and Cotton RG 10/3182, ff 39-40

38

ENUMERATION BOOK

FOR

* The Durham County Lunatic Asylum

Superintendent Registrar's District _Aycliffe_

Registrar's Sub-District _Sedgefield_

* Here insert the Name and Description of the Public Institution.

The above-mentioned Institution is situate within the Boundaries of the

† Parish [or Township] of	City or Municipal Borough of	Municipal Ward of	Parliamentary Borough of	Town [not being a City or Borough] of	Hamlet, or Tything, &c., of	Ecclesiastical District of
Sedgefield	‿	‿	‿	‿	‿	‿

† Draw the pen through such of the words as are inappropriate.

Title page to an institution.   RG 9/3696, f 38

Page 43

No.	NAME and SURNAME or Initials of Inmates	(1) RELATION to Head of Family—or (2) Position in the Institution	CONDITION	AGE MALES	AGE FEMALES	RANK, PROFESSION, or OCCUPATION	WHERE BORN	If Deaf-and-Dumb, or Blind
1	A.S. 215	Patient	Mar.?		55	Pauper	0	
2	A.B. 6	do	Mar.		63	Washerwoman	0	
3	A.W. 7	do	Single		45	?	0	
4	A.L. 8	do	Do		57	Factory Hand	0	
5	27 H 220	do	Mar.?	39		Labourer N.B.	0	
6	A.A. 1	do	Do		42	Ptman's wife	0	
7	A.J. 3	do	Single		45	Servant	0	
8	B.K. 4	do	Do		53	Dressmaker	0	
9	M.S. 5	do	Do		40	Tenant	0	
10	L.H. 6	do	Mar.?	49		Servant	0	
11	A.C. 9	do	?		49		0	
12	R.E. 230	do	Single	33		Ptman	0	
13	M.I. 1	do	Do		45	Pauper	0	
14	M.B. 3	do	Do		45	None	0	
15	S.B. 4	do	Do	34		Mariner	0	
16	L.D. 5	do	Widow	43		Joiner	0	
17	P.W. 6	do	Single	64		Pauper	0	
18	W.C. 7	do	Do	41		Pilot	0	
19	P.D. 8	do	Do			Seaman	0	
20	M.E. 9	do	Mar.?		26		0	
21	M.C. 240	do	Do	52		Mason's wife	0	
22	P.M. 1	do	Do		42	?	0	
23	S.D. 2	do	Single			Soldier	0	
24	P.M. 3	do	Do	67		Labourer	0	
25	P.R. 4	do	Do	35		Mariner	0	
	Total of Males and Females ...			9	16			

Completed page showing institutional entries.   RG 9/3696, f 43

To the MASTER or PERSON in CHARGE of the VESSEL.

1. You are requested to insert the particulars specified on the other side respecting all the persons who slept or abode on board the Vessel ON THE NIGHT OF APRIL 2nd, in compliance with an Act which passed the House of Commons and the House of Lords in the last Session of Parliament, and received the assent of Her Majesty The Queen on the 10th of August, 1870.

2. This Paper must be properly filled up ON THE MORNING OF APRIL 3rd, signed by yourself and delivered to the appointed Officer, who will apply to you for it.

[3. Should you be the MASTER of a BRITISH VESSEL and be out on the *night of April 2nd,* on a Coasting or short foreign voyage, you must fill up the Form on *April 3rd,* and deliver it with the *LEAST POSSIBLE DELAY either at the Custom House of the British Port of arrival,* or to the Officer who may apply for it.]

4. Persons who refuse to give correct information incur a penalty of Five Pounds.

5. The Return is required to enable the Secretary of State to complete the EIGHTH CENSUS, which is to show the exact numbers, ages, and conditions of the people—their arrangement in different ranks, professions, and trades—their distribution over sea and land—their increase and progress during the last ten years'

Approved,

H. A. BRUCE,

Home Office, Whitehall, Dec. 9th, 1870.

GEORGE GRAHAM,

Registrar General.

NUMBER of PERSONS belonging to the Vessel ON SHORE on the night of Sunday, APRIL 2nd :—

ABSENT ON SHORE. [Names not entered in the Schedule on the other side.]		
Males	Females	TOTAL.
Crew..............		
Passengers		
Total.....		

CENSUS
or
THE POPULATION,
1871.

SCHEDULE FOR VESSELS.

PREPARED UNDER THE DIRECTION OF ONE OF HER MAJESTY'S PRINCIPAL SECRETARIES OF STATE, PURSUANT TO THE ACT OF 33 & 34 VICT., c. 107.

NAME of VESSEL	Peace
Official Number (if any)	65.200
PORT or Place to which she belongs	Hull
Her Tonnage	40
Her DESCRIPTION, and the Trade in which she is employed	Smack Fishing Vessel
NAME of MASTER	Henry Bennett

Place at which the Schedule is delivered to the Master and the Date of Delivery.

Position of the Vessel at Midnight, April 2nd, 1871.

EXAMPLE of the MODE of FILLING UP the SCHEDULE.

	Name and Surname	Condition	Age of		Rank or Occupation	Where Born	If (1) Deaf-and-Dumb (2) Blind (3) Imbecile or Idiot (4) Lunatic
			Males	Females			
1	Alexander Fawcett	Married	42	...	Master	Durham, Sunderland	———
2	John Johnson	Married	34	...	Mate	Lanarkshire, Glasgow	———
3	George Saunders	Unmarried	25	...	A. B. Seaman	Yorkshire, Hull	———
4	Thomas Smith	Unmarried	21	...	O. Seaman	Middlesex, London	———
	[Here will follow all the Names of the Crew, Passengers, Visitors, and others].						
	Mary Fawcett	Married	...	35	Master's Wife	Yorkshire, Whitby	✓

Shipping schedule for the fishing smack 'Peace' from Hull.   RG 10/4797, f 134

Peace

134

LIST of OFFICERS, CREW, and OTHERS on BOARD of the SHIP or VESSEL, named the ___ on the NIGHT of SUNDAY, APRIL 2nd, 1871.

	NAME and SURNAME	CONDITION	AGE [Last Birthday] Males	AGE [Last Birthday] Females	RANK or OCCUPATION	WHERE BORN	If (1) Deaf-and-Dumb (2) Blind (3) Imbecile or Idiot (4) Lunatic
1	Henry Bennett	Married	37		Captain	Margate, Kent	
2	Henry Scott	Unmarried	42		Mate	London, Middlesex	
3	William Gerald		40		Fisherman	London, Middlesex	
4	John Richard Mallett		16		Fisherman	London, Middlesex	
5	Henry Wallis		15		Boy	Hull, Yorkshire	
6							
7							
8							
9							
10							
11							
12							
13							
14							
15							

I declare the foregoing to be a true Return, according to the best of my knowledge and belief.

Witness my Hand, Henry Bennett (Signature) Henry Bennett

Completed schedule for 'Peace'.   RG 10/4797, f 134

Remembering, therefore, that films for different years vary in their content, the following paragraphs explain each year's characteristics.

1841 Each film covers a series of small books. Each book has its own identifying number, marked on its first page. For example, piece HO 107/659 has books 659/1, 659/2 and so on. Each book has its own folio numbers on the top right-hand corner of every other page and may contain more than one enumeration district, the numbers of which are to be found on the title page of each district. This book number is also included on the identification slip which appears on the side or bottom of each frame of the film.

1851 Each piece has folio numbers which run right through the piece no matter how many separate books and enumeration districts are covered: they appear at the top right-hand corner of every other page. If a piece consists of more than one reel, the folio numbers covered by each reel are shown on the boxes. Wind on the film until you reach the folio numbers you were given in the reference books.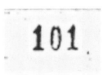

1861-1891 Each film covers a series of piece numbers which are foliated separately. Wind the film on to your piece number and look there for your place. If you have used a street index you can find your place by the folio numbers in the top right-hand corner of every other page, but some 1881 indexes don't give you folio numbers, just an enumeration district number, so turn to the enumerator's title page at the start of each district and look for your enumeration district number in the top right-hand corner. Then wind the film on and look for your street in that enumeration district.

Always make a careful note of reference numbers; it may be that you will need to refer to the same piece again in the future.

Charles Kean Tragedian HO 107/734, book 6 f 7 p 5

County of *Middlesex*

Hundred, Wapentake, Soke or Liberty of *Ossulstone*
Finsbury Division

Parish of *St James Clerkenwell p.d.*

Township of

City, Borough, Town or County Corporate of

Within the Limits of the Parliamentry Boundary
of the City or Borough of

Within the Municipal Boundary of

Superintendent Registrar's District of *St James Clerkenwell*

Registrar's District of *Amwell Clerkenwell*

No. of Enumeration District *1, 2 & 3*

Title page of book 5 for 1841 St James Clerkenwell.   HO 107/659, book 5 f 1

UNDERSTANDING THE RETURNS

The information supplied for each individual recorded in the 1841 census returns is name and age (rounded down to the nearest five years for people over fifteen, though this instruction is not always followed), occupation, and some indication of the area of birth. Relationship to the head of household may often be assumed from the sequence of names and ages, although in 1841 this is not recorded. Divisions between families on the page are shown thus / and divisions between dwellings are shown thus //.

The letters in the 'where born' column have the following meanings:

Y - yes = born in county of current residence
N - no = not born in county of current residence, but born in England or Wales
I = born in Ireland
S = born in Scotland
F = born abroad

The 'occupation' column may have the following abbreviations:

NK - not known
FS - female servant
MS - male servant

The returns for 1851, 1861, 1871, 1881 and 1891 are more informative. In addition to the information supplied in the 1841 returns, they give the exact ages of the persons enumerated, their marital status, relationship to the head of the household, and exact place of birth. The column on the extreme right is the disability column which records whether the individual is 'deaf and dumb', 'blind', and from 1871, an 'imbecile' or 'idiot' or 'lunatic'. This final column was not completed as frequently as it should have been (see E J Higgs, *Making Sense of the Census*, p 75). In one instance an enumerator has used the expression 'idiot' for the person's occupation (RG 9/2139, f 64 p 23). From 1891 returns from Welsh registration districts, and those for Monmouthshire, recorded whether a person was Welsh or English speaking or could speak both languages. For a sample of completed census pages for the years 1841 to 1891 see pp 45, 47, 49, 51, 53 -55. The returns for 29 Wharton Street show the mobility of the Victorian population.

Benjamin Disraeli Privy Councillor RG 9/43, f 65 p 12

PLACE	HOUSES		NAMES of each Person who abode therein the preceding Night.	AGE and SEX		PROFESSION, TRADE, EMPLOYMENT, or of INDEPENDENT MEANS.	Where Born	
	Uninhabited or Building	Inhabited		Males	Females		Whether Born in same County	Whether Born in Scotland, Ireland, or Foreign Parts.
Upper Wharton St			Emely Do		Month		Y	
			Eliza Rowe		15	F S ✓	N	
29		1	William Capper	30		Linen Draper	Y	
			Jane Do		30		N	
			Edward Do	2			Y	
			John Do		3 Month		Y	
			Mary Crunden		30	F S ✓	N	
			Ellen Olive		15	F S ✓	N	
30		1	Elizth Kennerley		30	Ind	N	
			Ellen Sullivan		25	F S ✓		I
Cumberland Cottage		1	Wm Turnidge	50		Porter ✓	N	
			Martha Do		50		N	
			Charlotte Do		10		N	
Cumberland Place No 1		1	Clarke Tomalin	50		Clerk ✓	N	
			Isabella Do		35		Y	
			Henry Do	15			N	
			Mary Mahigan		20	F S ✓		I
2		1	Joseph Wilson	30		Merchant	N	
			Joseph Do	1			Y	
			Sarah Singer		20	F S ✓	N	
3		1	Charles Rst	40		Ribbon M	Y	
			Ellen Connolly		25	F S ✓		I
4		1	Henry Dunster	55		Solicitor ✓	N	
			Richd Do	55		Accountant ✓	N	
			Frederick Do	20		Printer	N	
TOTAL in Page 19	7			11	14			

29 Wharton Street inhabited by William Capper, Linen Draper, and family. HO 107/659, book 5 f 40 p 19

45

Although the instructions issued to enumerators were very precise there are many instances where enumerators chose to stray from the rules and made observations or used unconventional terms to complete their returns. Title pages were intended to describe the district the enumerator had to cover but were also used by enumerators to add some comments of their own.

An enumerator in Beverley had carefully written out his instruction 'Enumerator must be careful and not take into the account any of the houses in St Nicholas Parish' and added 'Bow-Wow' (HO 107/2359, f 485). Others chose to voice their opinion on the neighbourhood they had been assigned: 'the houses marked marked thus x x x x in Close Alley are of a bad character consequently the information is doubtful the attention of the authorities has been directed towards them and several are closed' (RG 9/2455, f 67); and one lists the streets he covers with such remarks as 'all highly respectable, occupied chiefly by humble tradesmen, respectable shopkeepers' and so on (RG 9/5, f 90). One was so enthused with his district that he added 'I suppose a more laborious industrious and worthy community is not to be found within any other Enumerator's District' (RG 9/432, f 168). Another made the excuse 'this District being chiefly composed of the lower order of Irish such as an Lodging House Keepers, Pedlers, Rag Collectors, Chip Sellers, Bone Collectors, Hawkers of small wares, Beggers, etc. etc. I found it difficult to get at the proper description of some of the parties' (RG 9/2291, f 44). One concluded his summary with the poem:

So here you have the people all
From Brook Lane Farm to Puddingpoke Hall;
And here, in these mysterious pages,
You'll find the girls 'mysterious ages'.
The Sheep, the Wolves, in each vocation,
The Parson, Clerk & Congregation,
The Deaf, Dumb, Blind, the Wise, the Fools,
The Maids, Jades, Wives & Sunday Schools:
Publicans, Tailors, young Beginners,
Farmers & different sorts of Sinners.
Carpenters, wheelwrights & some Sawyers,
But free from Surgeons & from Lawyers!
Long life to all! and may the blushing maids
Next Census swell by splicing Brockford Blades!

(HO 107/1795, f 49 p iii)

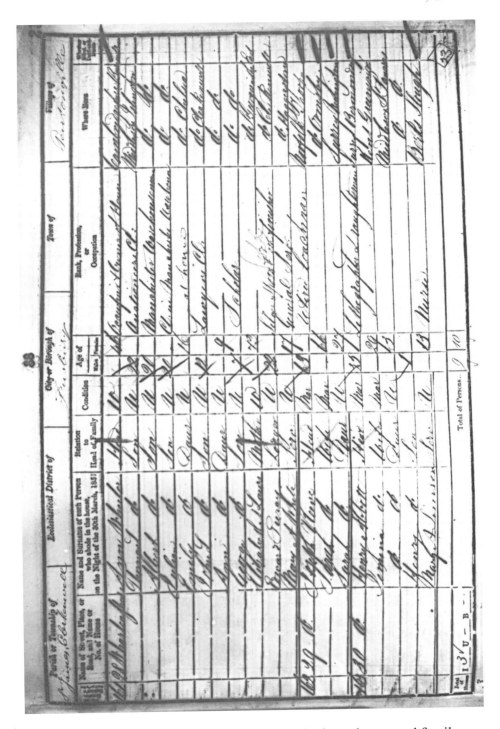

29 Wharton Street inhabited by Joseph Reeve, a retired coachman, and family.
HO 107/1517, f 23 p 38

Other comments made by enumerators relate mainly to the difficulties of gathering the information, but in one case the enumerator felt he had made a mistake in entering the information of a Merchant Navy establishment into his book: 'please see further on for Officers of the Institution which I see should have been entered first. I am sorry that I have been so stupid' (RG 10/3775, f 95 p 5). The problems of gathering information were expressed by an enumerator in Brightside: 'to ensure accuracy in my district I after delivering the Schedules visited nearly every house a second time. In addition to this on the 1st of April I sent the Bellman through the district to request the Household to fill up their schedules and to supply anyone who might have been omitted during my visit. He says he could not find an omission' (RG 10/4693, f 55). Another difficulty encountered was by an enumerator who said 'the omission of the place of birth in the case of the Lunatics are too frequent; but I was utterly at a loss to make them out from their incoherency' (RG 9/647, f 87 p 39). In spite of efforts made to provide correct information, the census officer queried the total of houses enumerated in relation to those mentioned by the enumerator; there should have been 400 inhabited houses but the enumerator had only accounted for 288. The local supervisor, when challenged, replied: 'Having seen the Enumerator, Mr Thomas Lilley, he stated to me that the Memorandum Book is correct, as he did it himself, but employed a Junior Clerk to fill up the Enumerator Book which will have Caused discrepencies. Now I may say that Mr Lilley had this same District last time, and I thought he would have done it the best of any, I am very much grieved he has not' (RG 9/3841, f 86). In RG 10/4899, f 66 of Yarm, Stockton, the enumerator, William Thompson, has calculated that he walked 25 miles in the course of 'Distributing the sheddles (sic)' and collecting them up again.

29 Wharton Street is uninhabited.   RG 9/192, f 70 p 20

Missing information: An enumerator in Manchester has explained the lack of information for one particular address by 'gross carelessness on the part of the Lodging Housekeeper. When I informed him to read the Schedule and told him of the penalty, it was all to no purpose, he said he asked their names and they would not tell him' (RG 10/4051, f 160 p 51). In another case an enumerator has explained 'consequent upon a general Row when tables were turned over, three forms were destroyed and the names of thirty-seven persons, all males, of ages varying from 19 to 60, were lost' (RG 11/322, f 35 p 16).

There is a note by a Superintendent Registrar: 'the foregoing sheets were filled up by the Reverend W J Palmer, the rector of Mixbury, but being incorect and Isaac Bayliss the Enumerator not being qualified for the Duty; W Thomas Hawkins of Brackley was apointed in his stead' (HO 107/ 886, book 12 f 13 p 21). Finally, there is evidence that one person was fined for refusing to give information: 'John Travers will not give any information respecting the persons who abode in his house on the night of June 6th only that the number was 125'. There is a note by the registrar that 'Mr Travers [was] fined £5 at the Mansion House by Sir Peter Lawrie June 23rd 1841' (HO 107/732, book 12 f 6 p 6).

29 Wharton Street inhabited by John Logan Grover, a solicitor, and his grandson. His housekeeper is not only a servant but is also the mother of his daughter-in-law! RG10/384, f 81 p 56

Doubts are often expressed that not everyone was included in the census and the remarks of one enumerator above prove this point. Efforts were made, however, to include even those people who had no address such as the three 'unknown men' recorded as 'heated by Japan stoves' in Aston in 1871 (RG 10/ 3138, f106 p 37) and George Johnson of Barton-upon-Irwell 'living in an empty coke oven' (RG 9/2859, f 74 p 17). George Jones of Hereford, although usually living in Catherine Street, was recorded as a labourer 'in search of work walking all night'.

One condition, though normally married, unmarried, or widowed, was 'widow bewitched' (RG 10/4407, f 89 p 30). Also listed were a changeling (RG 10/4563, f 82 p 13) and an orphan 'stolen when a child by gypsies' (RG 9/432, f 12 p 18).

Addresses were not always a precise house number and street name. You can find a gin palace (HO 107/1495, f 565 p 56), someone living in a shed whose relationship to the head of the family is simply 'friendly' (RG 9/1783, f 35 p 22) and 'a factory for beds uninhabited at night' (HO 107/1500, f 389 p 48).

The clerks who analysed the information had instructions on how to categorise the many occupations but some recorded must have caused them to scratch their heads as no categories had been provided for them. Amongst the usual means of employment are listed a 'professional wizard' (RG 10/4684, f 30 p 6), two fugitive slaves (HO 107/2321, f 530 p 27), just 'aristocratic' with the comment in another hand 'Oh Dear' (HO 107/ 2171, f 224 p 19), a squatter from Queensland (RG 11/140, f 28 p 49), a nymph of the pavé (HO 107/1508, f 578 p 36), a runaway slave (RG 9/4127, f 83 p 14) and those that defied even those unorthodox descriptions, 'nondescript' (RG 10/1299, f 21 p 14) and 'generally useful' (HO 107/ 1528, f 229 p 11).

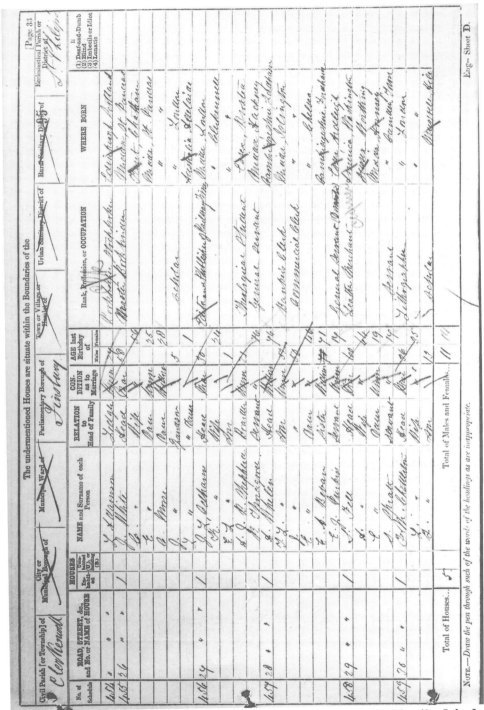

29 Wharton Street is now inhabited by S Fell, Leather Merchant, and family, John Logan Grover being deceased. RG 11/349, f 95 p 33

A title page of an 1891 return for Tunbridge Wells showing the signature of a female enumerator. The following enumeration district was enumerated by her brother and they themselves are enumerated on f 24.   RG 12/676, f 2 p i

29 Wharton Street has now been divided into two households.   RG 12/224, f 70 p 47

TO RETURN TO YOUR PLACE ON THE FILM

As you may need to refer to the entry again, you should note down the exact reference while the film is on the reader. You will need the reference number that you used to select the film, the folio number and the page number. You will also find this referencing system essential to enable you to pass on specific information about your research to other census users.

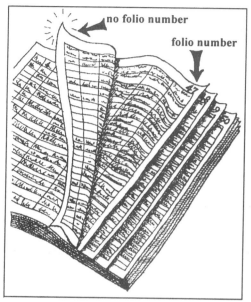

Before the original returns were microfilmed folio numbers were stamped on the top right-hand corner of every other page. The rule is that a page without a folio number is the reverse of the preceding page and therefore has the same folio number when quoted for reference. To refer to a specific page of a folio you only need to give the folio number and state whether it is the recto (first side or right side) or the verso (reverse side) of the folio. Many people, however, prefer to use page numbers to identify which side of the folio they are referring to. If you use this method beware of the many sequences of page numbering used in the census. The page numbers are printed on each page and are preceded by the word 'page' except for 1841 and 1851 when they appear in the centre and at the top of each page.

If your search is in the 1841 census you will also need a book number, because each piece covers a series of small books which have their identifying number marked on the first page and are foliated separately. It can be found on the reference strip on the side or on the bottom of the frame.

Having found what you want, make a note of the folio and page number and then roll back the film to the first folio of that sequence, where you will find folio '1', and look at the

bottom of that page, which will have a figure like a fraction with the piece number above and the book number below. The book number is also noted on the reference strip on the side or the bottom of each frame of the film. Check that you have correctly recorded these two numbers.

William Gladstone MP HO 107/739, book 3 f 8 p 8

USING A MICROFICHE READER

To use a microfiche reader you need to collect the card on the front of each reader and put in place of the fiche you have selected from the stands on the table. To insert the fiche into the reader, pull the plate on which it sits towards you and the glass cover will rise enabling you to place the fiche under it. You need to insert the fiche with the fiche header on the edge nearest to you. Push back the plate unit and the image will appear on the screen. The plate slides to and fro and up and down to enable you to move from frame to frame. If the image is unclear adjust the focus knobs. There is also a black lever which enables you to change the magnification if you prefer. When you put the fiche away, don't forget to replace the card on the reader for the next person.

PHOTOCOPIES

If you would like a photocopy of part of the census returns, before removing the film from the microfilm reader you need to identify the frame of film you require (note that poor quality originals or scratched films will not reproduce high quality copies).

If you are unsure as to how to identify the correct frame, **leave the film on your reader, switch the reader off, and consult an officer.**

To obtain photocopies you need to know the full reference number including:

1841 - the book number and the folio number, eg:

HO 107/659,   book 5, folio 3   HO 107 / 659 / 5

1851-1891 - the folio number and the page number, eg:

HO 107/1595	folio 243 page 29
RG 9/1053	folio 136 page 1
RG 10/653	folio 122 page 6
RG 11/1253	folio 43 page 12
RG 12/456	folio 29 page 16

See also appendix 4.

George Du Maurier Artist 'Punch' RG 11/166, f 99 p 19

Postal applications for photocopies must have full correct references including folio numbers and page numbers.

There is one other factor you should consider if you plan to reproduce a document (ie to quote substantial parts of it or to print photographs or other copies of it). All census returns are subject to Crown copyright (see appendix 3).

Please note that surname indexes other than the 1881 surname index and the IGI cannot be photocopied. They are the copyright of the family history societies who compiled them and application should be made to the appropriate society.

To obtain a copy from film or fiche you can either make a copy yourself or ask a member of staff to produce the copy which will cost a little more. In order to pay for the self-service copies you will need to purchase a copy card from the Copy Desk. Once the card has been used you can recharge it by putting coins in the slot adjacent to the copy machines which are located at various points round the edge of the Reading Room.

Cost per copy

With cash
With card

- Purchase card from copy desk

- To recharge your card either:

  Insert card, press green button, insert coins

  or

  Take card to copy desk (cash, cheque, credit card)

- To remove card press green button

Please note that this machine will only take plastic cards and not the ones issued at Chancery Lane.

Microform Reader/Printers

Machines to make copies from fiche are labelled fiche only.

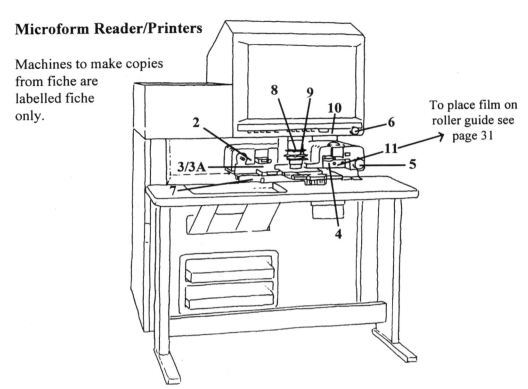

To place film on roller guide see page 31

Instructions for fiche only

1) Pull fiche carriage towards you, place fiche between the two pieces of glass and push the carriage back in place.
2) If the image is back to front take out the fiche, turn it over, and replace it between the pieces of glass.
3) If the image is upside down or off at an angle use the rotation knob to straighten it up the right way.
4) Select either A4 or A3.
5) Move the carriage so that the frames you wish to copy appear on the screen. If A3 is selected, the whole screen will be copied. If A4 is selected only the middle section of the screen will be copied.
6) Use the zoom lens to enlarge or reduce the image.
7) Focus the image.
8) Place either a copycard or cash into the Cashkard machine located to the side of the copier (please note that no change can be given.
9) Press green print button to make a copy.

Instructions for using ABR 2700 (film) copier

BLACK LOCATION NUMBER	OPERATING INSTRUCTIONS FOR PRINTS FROM MICROFILM
1	Place photocopy unit card in Emos card system slot.
2	Place film on left hand spindle.
3	Feed the microfilm trailer into the green film guide by pressing the green button to lift up black bridge.
3A	Feed film through to far side and push down black bridge.
4	Press the load/rewind key.
5	Advance film with speed control knob. To slowly advance the microfilm, turn knob partially.
6	Use image rotation knob if required.
7	Position image on the screen by moving scanning lever as required.
8	Zoom lens.
9	Focus the image with focus control.
	TO PRINT A COPY
10	Press the green print button.
11	Rewind the microfilm on original spool by pressing the rewind button.

PROBLEMS AND HOW TO SOLVE THEM

MISPLACING YOUR NOTEBOOK

It is a good idea to put your name and address in the front of your notebook. Nothing is more soul-destroying than to leave it somewhere knowing that you will not be revisiting that place for a few weeks. The Census Room staff will automatically return notebooks that have an address inside the cover.

FAILING TO RECORD REFERENCES

Another good practice that may not become apparent until you are well into your research is to **keep an exact reference** of every search you have done, even if it is unsuccessful. It will save hours of duplicate searching when a year or two later you are planning what to look at next and need to remember exactly what you have already examined. It will also be invaluable to relations researching other branches of your family (see appendix 4).

MISSING INFORMATION

Families

If families do not appear where expected there are various possible explanations.

There was some deliberate evasion of the enumerators. Turner, the painter, for instance, is reputed to have spent census night on a boat on the Thames to avoid being enumerated. Evasion was, however, more usually practised among the lowest ranks of society and especially by criminals.

Working class families appear to have moved from house to house with surprising frequency, and the address taken from a birth or marriage certificate may be out-of-date a few months later.

Many more people leased their houses than do now. This meant that they moved frequently when leases ran out. However, they most probably needed to be within easy walking distance of the same job. If you cannot find a family at a particular address look round the neighbourhood; they may not be far away.

Henry Irving Comedian RG 11/95, f 31 p 19

Charles Dickens is to be found staying with Robert Davey a medical practitioner at 34 Kepple Street, St George, Bloomsbury. He is listed as 'a visitor aged 39 author born Portsmouth, Hants' and with him, also visitors, are 'Alfred Samuel Dickens married 29 an engineer born Chatham, Kent and Augustus Newsham Dickens married 23 a merchants clerk born London'.

HO 107/1507, f 206 p 16

His family, but not his wife, are to be found at their home 1 Devonshire Terrace in Marylebone. Mary Dickens aged 12 is described in the column headed 'Relationship to Head of Household' as daughter of Charles Dickens and her occupation is again 'Daughter of Charles Dickens'. With her are listed Catherine, 11, Francis, 7, Alfred, 5, Sidney Smith, 4, Henry, 2, and Dora Ann 8 months, with a cook, wetnurse, and nurse.

HO 107/1488, f 207 p 9

Mrs Dickens is away from home and can be found staying in a Lodging House with her sister at Knotsford Lodge, Great Malvern whilst, presumably, taking the waters. The entry reads: 'Catherine Dickens lodger married 35 born Edinburgh and her sister Georgina Hogarth lodger unmarried 24 born Edinburgh'.

HO 107/2043, f 98 p 21

The people you are looking for might not have been at home on census night, in which case they will appear at the address where they were staying. In the 1851 census the Dickens family are a very good example of this.

Films

1.   Folio numbers may be missing from the sequence: this means that the folio was missed when filming. In this case ask the officer if it is possible to see the original or, where this is not possible, to have the original checked for you.

2.   If page numbers are missing from the sequence (but the foliation is correct) the folio did not survive. This situation most often occurs at the back or front of a book which has lost its covers. Unfortunately there is no solution. Another census year should be tried.

3.   Some places are missing from the films: these are described as 'MISSING' in the class lists. There is no solution as the enumerators' books disappeared before the returns were transferred to the Public Record Office.

Items missing from indexes

Streets missing from the indexes suggest a number of possibilities:

the street had not yet been built;
the street was being built at the time;
the street was not yet named as such and the houses
  are identified by the name of villas, terraces, etc;
the street was missed by the indexers;
or the folio did not survive and so could not have been
  indexed.

If this happens in a London index look in Book 91 or 92 (see 6 (ii) p 21) to find the date of approval of the street name or the name of the villas, terraces, etc from which the street was formed. If this does not provide a satisfactory answer then try the street index for another year, and determine at least the sub-district into which it falls; otherwise find another street with the same reference as the street you seek. Then look up the same sub-district or other street in the year you are researching and check the film in case the individual houses or actual street appear in that part of the film and have been missed or disguised in the index.

Items missing from microfilms

1.   Houses may be missing from streets: many streets were not numbered until long after they were built and were composed of named villas, terraces, cottages, buildings or individual houses which later remained under those names but were also numbered as part of the longer 'mother street'. Such houses may feature in the index under their former names.

2.   Numbers are often missing from streets, since the numerical sequence of houses was erratic in the last century; on the other hand some streets had as many as four separate sequences of house numbers. At a later date this may have been rationalised, but it sometimes pays to continue looking through all references to a street in case the people you seek are indeed living at the house number you expect, but not at the particular house you are looking at because that has a duplicate number. In other words, there might be another 5 Hallam Street further on in the enumeration district. However, not all enumerators bothered to record house numbers and just entered the name of the road.

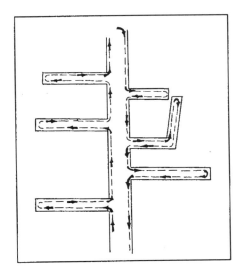

3.   If house numbers are apparently missing from their sequence, this is because house numbers do not necessarily appear in sequence. The enumerator probably took the shortest route through his district. He may have begun at one end of a street (not necessarily number 1), walked down to the next crossroads, turned into a side street, then continued with the first street, ending up finally with number 1 when he reached the end of his rounds several crossroads later, on the other side of the street in which he started.

If only even, or only odd, numbers are recorded it probably indicates that the street was incomplete and only one side was built. It can also mean, however, that one side of the street was in one enumeration district and the other side of the street was in the next enumeration district, or even that the street was split between

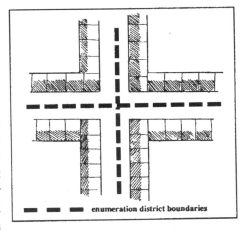

- - - enumeration district boundaries

several enumeration districts where the boundaries of an enumeration district occur at crossroads. The street index will cross refer you to other parts of the census where the rest of the street occurs.

Francis Reckitt Manufacturer of Starches, Blues, Black Lead, and of Machine and Fancy Biscuits by Steam RG 9/3592, f 75

In large towns, especially in the Midlands, you will find named buildings and courts listed in the street index. This is where an alleyway leading off a street opens into a courtyard round the sides of which are numerous dwellings, probably several storeys high.

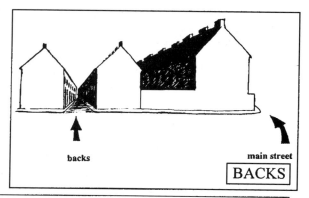

BACKS

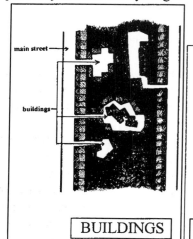

BUILDINGS

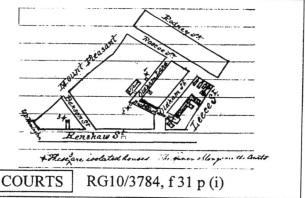

COURTS RG10/3784, f 31 p (i)

SUBJECT OF ENQUIRY IN OLDHAM REGISTRATION DISTRICT
Enumeration District 16
From Mr William Ascroft to Mr James L Page, enumerator
Please give a description of the premises designated "Cellar Dwellings" in the Memorandum Book of this District -
Whether they are Cellars <u>under Houses</u> or separate and distinct habitations called "<u>Cellar Dwellings</u>" -
Please return the Memorandum Book (5 September 1861)
Answer
In answer to your inquiry the term Cellar Dwellings applies to Dwellings under houses in cases where the Ground floor of the Houses are level with the front Street and the Floor of Cellars under the Ground floors are level with a Back Street. The Houses (so called) and the Cellar Dwellings (so called) being in the occupation of seperate tenants - I may somewhat elucidate the matter by saying that the Front Streets have been raised, after the original construction of the Streets and the erection of the Houses: <u>to avoid great declivities</u> and Render the ascent to various parts of the Town easier whilst the Section of the Surface of the Land at the Back has been left in its original State - Afterwards advantage has been taken of making seperate dwellings to face front and back. <u>No connexion existing between such seperate dwellings</u>.

RG 9/3010, f 51

HOUSES	
In-	Unin-
1	
	2U
1	

4.   If families are missing from houses, they may have been away from home on census night. The purpose of the census survey was to record not only individuals but also buildings, and thus the building in which they normally lived would have been recorded as 'uninhabited'.

If a house was uninhabited on census night it will still be enumerated but will probably be identifiable only by its place between two others. There is a column for uninhabited houses on the enumerator's form.

Missing places: Places missing from a class list means that a particular part of the census did not survive; another year should be tried. Places may be missing from a place-name index because the place being sought may be the name of an ecclesiastical parish instead of the civil parish on which the census was based. The List of Parishes (Book 94) should provide the answer (see 6 (iv) p 22). It lists most place names and in the second column on the page it will tell you in which civil parish they occur. Smaller places than a civil parish can be difficult to locate in the 1891 census. The newly designed title pages enabled the enumerator to break down his allotted patch into various administrative divisions, parts of which would be in his enumeration district and parts in other enumeration districts. Most can be ignored when searching the returns as the civil parish is the most useful unit for identifying a place in census terms. However, it is very often a township, village or hamlet within this civil parish that one needs to identify. At first glance this breakdown of places on the title page makes this identification easier. However, when you turn to the pages which follow, the box headings are frequently, but luckily not always, ignored by the enumerator which means that location of a particular hamlet or township is impossible unless you happen to know the names of the streets in that hamlet.

Birthplaces: As far as the place of birth entry is concerned, you should remember that many people did not know where they were born, and some others lied about it, fearing that the information might be used to send them back to their home parish, as the Poor Law directed.

Some enumerators, being local men, would not know the place names of the part of the country whence the person they interviewed came. This, combined with a 'foreign' local accent, might produce a place-name spelling that will not occur in any gazetteer or map. If this happens try pronouncing the name given as a local might have done. Perhaps the 'H' has been missed at the beginning.

Ages: Ages given in the returns are not always reliable; some people did not know exactly when they were born and there were many reasons for lying about one's age.

HOW TO INDEX THE RETURNS

At first sight there is a bewildering variety of census indexes; but they fall into clearly defined categories as already noted (see 'Using the Finding Aids' above). The first place to look is in the place-name index for your particular census year, or go to a street index if this is more appropriate. Copies of these indexes are provided by the PRO.

However, family history societies have, for the past decade, been busy compiling another type of index. Different researchers need different pieces of information, and family historians need names before they need places. Transcripts are never really necessary unless the document is not to be made available because it is fragile; researchers should always check an original source rather than rely on someone else's translation or interpretation, which can, even with the best intentions, go astray. It is far more sensible, therefore, to compile an index only. The recommended minimum content for a census index is surname, forename, age, birthplace and reference. If some uniformity is applied to census indexing it will be possible in the future to combine local indexes into a national one, which will be far easier to use. The Public Record Office has several surname indexes that have most generously been donated by family history societies, and more would be appreciated.

Anyone planning to index census returns for publication should adopt the method of referencing used in the Census Room. Then, anyone quoting a reference or placing an order for a photocopy at the Public Record Office, or asking for help in deciphering entries, would be talking the same 'language'. Searchers are frequently asked by the Census Room staff to return to their local record office or library and look again at the film to find the reference required since the information given is insufficient to locate the precise entry at the PRO. All this is time wasting. Individual methods of indexing, while appropriate in the smaller context of a local record office or library, are inadequate when applied to the holdings in the PRO, and it is vital that the complete PRO reference, including the folio and page number, is quoted, though you may find it easier to use the archival terms recto and verso instead of a page number (see also page 56 for folio numbers and page 57 for examples of complete references). All the original enumerators' books are foliated before being microfilmed, which means that one can go straight to the page required, but frequently the folio numbers are disregarded by indexers (see page 56).

Another important factor to consider when planning a census project is the area covered by the index. The census has its own in-built natural divisions for ease of enumeration. It is sensible, therefore, to use these divisions when defining the size of the index. The easiest unit to use, from a searcher's point of view, is that of the registration district. If this is too large to manage then an index to a sub-district is a suitable alternative. Both

---

Byron Family Baron Byron BA RG 11/95, f 29 p 15

of these units will be more than one piece number (the archival term for an individual item and the third element of your reference number) and some people do index one piece number only. This can be confusing to a user of the index because it is not easy to define just one piece as being part of a whole. Worse still, some indexers choose a parish as a unit for indexing. Not only does this sometimes mean that you need to index part of a piece number, but also many searchers are unaware of the fact that census parishes are civil ones and 'parish' in its usual form refers to an ecclesiastical district. The question arises, 'which type of parish is being indexed?' When providing an index, therefore, to a particular set of documents it is much more user-friendly to remain within the natural framework of the documents themselves.

1881 CENSUS PROJECT

The British Genealogical Record Users Committee (an informal group with representatives from the Federation of Family History Societies, the Society of Genealogists, the

Institute of Genealogical and Heraldic Studies, the Public Record Office, and the Genealogical Society of Utah among others) have made the 1881 census the object of a national indexing project.

To avoid duplication of effort because so much work had already been done on the 1851 census, it was decided to concentrate on the 1881 census for England and Wales. The thirty-year gap in time between the two will help a new generation of researchers for whom the 1881 census will provide essential information at the beginning of their work.

The Genealogical Society of Utah (GSU) organised the work that needed to be done to get all twenty-six million names of the accompanying information onto fiche, the bulk of the labour force being supplied by member societies of the Federation of Family History Societies.

The resulting data has been made available on microfiche, both as a full transcript of the returns and as indexes to them. The three indexes are all arranged by county then by surname within the county; by surnames of people born in the same parish; or by surnames within a place being enumerated. This can be seen in the reading room. The Family History Societies provide photocopies of entries found by the indexes from their area and soon the whole project will be available on CD-ROM. No other census is so easily accessible.

The first and last of WILLIALL taking the Causes of England & Wales unless the price goes up.

Alpha & Omega

RG 10/1313, f 43 p 44.   Not all enumerators were happy in their work!

APPENDIX 1   DATES AND POPULATION

The dates for the taking of the census are as follows:

1841	June 6	Population of 15,914,000
1851	March 30	Population of 17,928,000
1861	April 7	Population of 20,066,000
1871	April 2	Population of 22,723,000
1881	April 3	Population of 25,974,000
1891	April 5	Population of 28,999,725

APPENDIX 2   CENSUS DIVISIONS

1   London within LCC boundaries; see map opposite

2   South Eastern - Surrey and Kent (extra-metropolitan),
            Sussex, Hampshire, Berkshire

3   South Midland - Middlesex (extra-metropolitan),
            Hertfordshire, Buckinghamshire, Oxfordshire, Northamptonshire,
            Huntingdonshire, Bedfordshire, Cambridgeshire

4   Eastern - Essex, Suffolk, Norfolk

5   South Western - Wiltshire, Dorset, Devon, Cornwall and
            Somerset

6   West Midland - Gloucestershire, Herefordshire, Shropshire,
            Staffordshire, Worcestershire, Warwickshire

7   North Midland - Leicestershire, Rutland,
            Lincolnshire, Nottinghamshire, Derbyshire

8   North Western - Cheshire, Lancashire

9   Yorkshire

10   Northern - County Durham, Northumberland,
            Cumberland, Westmorland

11   Welsh - Monmouthshire and
            Wales

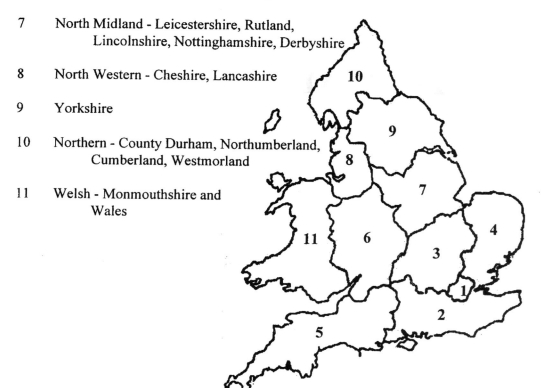

Division 1

1	Kensington	19	London City
2	Chelsea	20	Shoreditch
3	St George Hanover Square	21	Bethnal Green
4	Westminster	22	Whitechapel
5	St Martin in the Fields	23	St George in the East
6	St James Westminster	24	Stepney
7	Marylebone	25	Poplar
8	Hampstead	26	St Saviour Southwark
9	Pancras	27	St Olave Southwark
10	Islington	28	Bermondsey
11	Hackney	29	St George Southwark
12	St Giles	30	Newington
13	Strand	31	Lambeth
14	Holborn	32	Wandsworth
15	Clerkenwell	33	Camberwell
16	St Luke	34	Rotherhithe
17	East London	35	Greenwich
18	West London	36	Lewisham

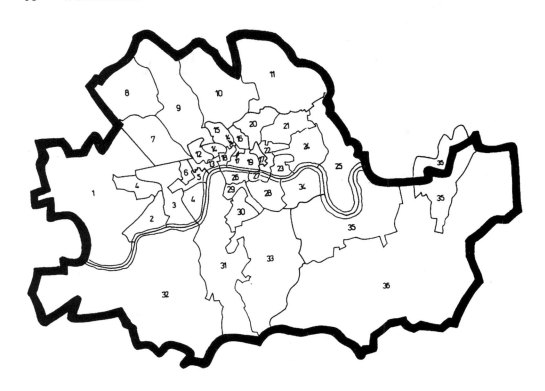

APPENDIX 3   COPYRIGHT IN CENSUS RETURNS

All British census returns are Crown copyright. Unauthorised reproduction of the returns - whether in facsimile or transcript - may infringe copyright.

1.   Making copies from microfilms

The Public Record Office has no objection to the reproduction of limited quantities of hard copy print from microfilms of the census returns held by local libraries, family history societies, and other non-profit-making organisations. It is perfectly acceptable for holders of such microfilms to supply, for example:

a) single copies of isolated pages to individuals for purposes of research or private study;

b) single copies of consecutive pages covering an area of one complete parish, to local or family history societies or individuals, for purposes of academic or other non-commercial research including the compilation of indexes to the returns;

c) multiple copies of isolated or small numbers of consecutive pages, to teachers or lecturers, for use with classes in schools or as part of a higher or adult education programme.

2.   Publishing facsimiles and transcripts of the returns

Requests for permission to publish parts of the returns, in facsimile or transcript, should be addressed to the Copyright Officer at the Public Record Office, who will, in most instances, be able to give permission for the project. The PRO reserves the right to levy Crown copyright reproduction fees, although such fees are not normally charged for non-profit-making publications by individuals or by family and local history societies. Proposals for publication on a large or commercial scale, and proposals to reproduce the contents of the returns for distribution in machine readable form, may be referred to Her Majesty's Stationery Office, which bears ultimate responsibility for the administration of Crown copyright.

Requests for permission to publish should be made in writing, and should always include full details of the proposed publication, and the PRO document reference(s) of the returns concerned. These references are clearly visible on all microfilm copies of the census returns.

3.   Publishing indexes to the returns

Permission is not always required for the publication of indexes to the returns. Copyright is infringed only if the information in the returns is reproduced exactly, or so completely that the new work becomes a substitute for the originals. This means that there is no potential infringement, and hence no need for permission, if all that is to be published is a simple index which serves only as a finding aid to the returns. An example of this would be a surname index referring users to a particular entry, which they would then need to consult on microfilm for full details.

N.B. Any work which contains all the information given in the original returns counts as full reproduction for which permission is required, even if the information has been rearranged in the transcript (eg in alphabetical order of surname).

4.   The 1881 Microfiche Project

Two distinct copyrights subsist in the microfiche indexes to the 1881 census. The data from the returns are Crown copyright: copyright in the indexes themselves, including their arrangement and layout, belongs to the Corporation of the President, the Church of Jesus Christ of the Latter-Day Saints. Both copyright owners are happy that limited numbers of copies (both fiche and hard copy) should be made from the microfiche edition, in the quantities and for the purposes outlined in paragraph 1 above. Requests for permission to produce or obtain more extensive quantities of copies, or for permission to publish any portion of the indexes in facsimile or transcript, should be addressed in the first instance to the copyright officer of the Church. Some requests may be referred subsequently to HM Stationery Office.

APPENDIX 4   DOCUMENT REFERENCES

Reference numbers are needed to identify specific documents, not just census returns, and have three component parts. The first is the letter code to the group of documents into which your particular document falls. This letter code relates to the government department which transferred the document. In the case of the census this is HO (Home Office) for 1841 and 1851 and RG (Registrar General) for all other years.

The second part is a class number, since each group of documents is subdivided into classes relating to different types of documents all being transferred from the same source. To cite an example, the classes of the RG group are as follows: RG 1-3 are the indexes to the birth, marriage and death registers still held by the Office of National Statistics; RG 4 nonconformist registers (gathered in 1837); RG 5 certificates of Dr Williams' Library; RG 6 Quaker registers; RG 7 Fleet marriage registers; RG 8 unauthenticated nonconformist registers (gathered in 1857); RG 9 1861 census returns; RG 10 1871 census returns; RG 11 1881 census returns; RG 12 1891 census returns and so on. RG 18 reference maps of registrar's districts, RG 19 correspondence and papers, RG 27 specimens of forms and documents and RG 30 reports and population abstracts, are some of the later classes.

The third part of the reference is what is known as a piece number. This is simply an archival term for an individual item which may take many shapes and forms, but which when relating to the census means an enumerator's folder or in 1841 and 1851 a box of these folders.

To complete a reference you need to add the particular folio number or numbers followed by either recto or verso, or a page number. See page 56 for a fuller explanation of this.

These document references are universal in that they are present on a reel of census microfilm wherever you view it. However, if you are looking at the census away from the PRO in a local record office or a family history library, you will not have the same finding aids available to identify your part of the census in the same way. Quite naturally other search rooms have their own collections and will need to add any purchased microfilms to their own holdings. This means that a new reference will need to be applied to any item purchased by them in order for it to be added to their referencing system. Local record offices in particular may have also purchased copies of street indexes, where available, from the PRO so that PRO references can be used in conjunction with their own system. Taking with you to another record office a PRO reference number may therefore necessitate an extra exercise before you can find your film. The local archivist or search room officer should be able to help you do this. Once you have found your place on the film you will be able to refer back to it by the method described on page 56. Similarly the local referencing system will not be intelligible away from its own collection so you will need the PRO reference for what you wish to record to make it universally intelligible.

APPENDIX 5   REGISTRATION DISTRICTS

London Division 1

1851	1861	1871	1881	1891
pt Kensington	pt Kensington	pt Kensington	pt Kensington	1A Paddington
1 Kensington	1 Kensington	1 Kensington	1 Kensington	1B Kensington
pt Kensington	pt Kensington	pt Kensington	2 Fulham	2 Fulham
2 Chelsea	2 Chelsea	2 Chelsea	3 Chelsea	3 Chelsea
3 St George Hanover Sq	3 St George Hanover Sq	3 St George Hanover Sq	4 St George Hanover Sq	4 St George Hanover Sq
4 Westminster	4 Westminster	4 Westminster	5 Westminster	pt Westminster
Westminster				
5 St Martin in the Fields	5 St Martin in the Fields	pt Westminster	pt Westminster	pt Westminster
6 St James Westminster	6 St James Westminster	pt Westminster	pt Westminster	
7 Marylebone	7 Marylebone	5 Marylebone	6 Marylebone	6 Marylebone
8 Hampstead	8 Hampstead	6 Hampstead	7 Hampstead	7 Hampstead
9 Pancras	9 Pancras	7 Pancras	8 Pancras	8 Pancras
10 Islington	10 Islington	8 Islington	9 Islington	9 Islington
11 Hackney	11 Hackney	9 Hackney	10 Hackney	10 Hackney
12 St Giles	12 St Giles	10 St Giles	11 St Giles	11 St Giles
13 Strand	13 Strand	11 Strand	12 Strand	12 Strand
14 Holborn	14 Holborn	12 Holborn	13 Holborn	13 Holborn
15 Clerkenwell	15 Clerkenwell	pt Holborn	pt Holborn	pt Holborn
16 St Luke	16 St Luke	pt Holborn	pt Holborn	pt Holborn
17 E London	17 E London	pt London City	pt London City	pt London City
18 W London	18 W London	pt London City	pt London City	pt London City
19 London City	19 London City	13 London City	14 London City	14 London City
20 Shoreditch	20 Shoreditch	14 Shoreditch	15 Shoreditch	15 Shoreditch
21 Bethnal Green	21 Bethnal Green	15 Bethnal Green	16 Bethnal Green	16 Bethnal Green
22 Whitechapel	22 Whitechapel	16 Whitechapel	17 Whitechapel	17 Whitechapel
23 St George in the East	23 St George in the East	17 St George in the East	18 St George in the East	18 St George in the East
24 Stepney	24A Stepney	18 Stepney	19 Stepney	19 Stepney
pt Stepney	24B Mile End Old Town	19 Mile End Old Town	20 Mile End Old Town	20 Mile End Old Town

	1851	1861	1871	1881	1891	
London Division 1	25	25 Poplar	20 Poplar	21 Poplar	21 Poplar	
	26	26 St Saviour Southwark	21 St Saviour Southwark	22 St Saviour Southwark	22 St Saviour Southwark	
	27	27 St Olave Southwark	22 St Olave Southwark	23 St Olave Southwark	23 St Olave Southwark	
			pt St Olave	pt St Olave	pt St Olave	
			pt St Saviour	pt St Saviour	pt St Saviour	
			pt St Saviour	pt St Saviour	pt St Saviour	
	28	28 Bermondsey				
	29	29 St George Southwark				
	30	30 Newington				
	31	31 Lambeth	23 Lambeth	24 Lambeth	24 Lambeth	
	32	32 Wandsworth	24 Wandsworth	25 Wandsworth	25 Wandsworth	
	33	33 Camberwell	25 Camberwell	26 Camberwell	26 Camberwell	
	34	34 Rotherhithe	pt St Olave	pt St Olave	pt St Olave	
	35	35 Greenwich	26 Greenwich	27 Greenwich	27 Greenwich	
	36	36 Lewisham	27 Lewisham	28 Lewisham	28 Lewisham	
		pt Greenwich	28 Woolwich	29 Woolwich	29 Woolwich	
Surrey	37	37 Epsom	29 Epsom	30 Epsom	30 Epsom	
	38	38 Chertsey	30 Chertsey	31 Chertsey	31 Chertsey	
	39	39 Guildford	31 Guildford	32 Guildford	32 Guildford	
	40	40 Farnham	32 Farnham	33 Farnham	33 Farnham	
	41	41 Farnborough	pt Hartley Wintney	pt Hartley Wintney	pt Hartley Wintney	
	42	42 Hambledon	33 Hambledon	34 Hambledon	34 Hambledon	
	43	43 Dorking	34 Dorking	35 Dorking	35 Dorking	
	44	44 Reigate	35 Reigate	36 Reigate	36 Reigate	
	45	45 Godstone	36 Godstone	37 Godstone	37 Godstone	
	46	46 Croydon	37 Croydon	38 Croydon	38 Croydon	
	47	47 Kingston	38 Kingston	39 Kingston	39 Kingston	
	48	48 Richmond	39 Richmond	40 Richmond	40 Richmond	
	49	49 Bromley	40 Bromley	41 Bromley	41 Bromley	
	50	50 Dartford	41 Dartford	42 Dartford	42 Dartford	
	51	51 Gravesend	42 Gravesend	43 Gravesend	43 Gravesend	

1851		1861		1871		1881		1891	
52	North Aylesford	52	North Aylesford	43	North Aylesford	44	North Aylesford	44	Strood
53	Hoo	53	Hoo	44	Hoo	45	Hoo	45	Hoo
54	Medway	54	Medway	45	Medway	46	Medway	46	Medway
55	Malling	55	Malling	46	Malling	47	Malling	47	Malling
56	Sevenoaks	56	Sevenoaks	47	Sevenoaks	48	Sevenoaks	48	Sevenoaks
57	Tonbridge	57	Tonbridge	48	Tonbridge	49	Tonbridge	49	Tonbridge
58	Maidstone	58	Maidstone	49	Maidstone	50	Maidstone	50	Maidstone
59	Hollingbourne	59	Hollingbourne	50	Hollingbourne	51	Hollingbourne	51	Hollingbourne
60	Cranbrook	60	Cranbrook	51	Cranbrook	52	Cranbrook	52	Cranbrook
61	Tenterden	61	Tenterden	52	Tenterden	53	Tenterden	53	Tenterden
62	West Ashford	62	West Ashford	53	West Ashford	54	West Ashford	54	West Ashford
63	East Ashford	63	East Ashford	54	East Ashford	55	East Ashford	55	East Ashford
64	Bridge	64	Bridge	55	Bridge	56	Bridge	56	Bridge
65	Canterbury	65	Canterbury	56	Canterbury	57	Canterbury	57	Canterbury
66	Blean	66	Blean	57	Blean	58	Blean	58	Blean
67	Faversham	67	Faversham	58	Faversham	59	Faversham	59	Faversham
68	Milton	68	Milton	59	Milton	60	Milton	60	Milton
69	Sheppey	69	Sheppey	60	Sheppey	61	Sheppey	61	Sheppey
70	Thanet	70	Thanet	61	Thanet	62	Thanet	62	Thanet
71	Eastry	71	Eastry	62	Eastry	63	Eastry	63	Eastry
72	Dover	72	Dover	63	Dover	64	Dover	64	Dover
73	Elham	73	Elham	64	Elham	65	Elham	65	Elham
74	Romney Marsh	74	Romney Marsh	65	Romney Marsh	66	Romney Marsh	66	Romney Marsh	**Kent**
75	Rye	75	Rye	66	Rye	67	Rye	67	Rye
76	Hastings	76	Hastings	67	Hastings	68	Hastings	68	Hastings
77	Battle	77	Battle	68	Battle	69	Battle	69	Battle
78	Eastbourne	78	Eastbourne	69	Eastbourne	70	Eastbourne	70	Eastbourne
79	Hailsham	79	Hailsham	70	Hailsham	71	Hailsham	71	Hailsham	**Sussex**

Sussex

1851	1861	1871	1881	1891
80 Ticehurst	80 Ticehurst	71 Ticehurst	72 Ticehurst	72 Ticehurst
81 Uckfield	81 Uckfield	72 Uckfield	73 Uckfield	73 Uckfield
82 East Grinstead	82 East Grinstead	73 East Grinstead	74 East Grinstead	74 East Grinstead
83 Cuckfield	83 Cuckfield	74 Cuckfield	75 Cuckfield	75 Cuckfield
84 Lewes	84 Lewes	75 Lewes	76 Lewes	76 Lewes
85 Brighton	85 Brighton	76 Brighton	77 Brighton	77 Brighton
86 Steyning	86 Steyning	77 Steyning	78 Steyning	78 Steyning
87 Horsham	87 Horsham	78 Horsham	79 Horsham	79 Horsham
88 Petworth	88 Petworth	79 Petworth	80 Petworth	80 Petworth
89 Thakeham	89 Thakeham	80 Thakeham	81 Thakeham	81 Thakeham
pt Worthing	pt Worthing	81 East Preston	82 East Preston	82 East Preston
90 Worthing	90 Worthing	pt East Preston	pt East Preston	pt East Preston
91 Westhampnett	91 Westhampnett	82 Westhampnett	83 Westhampnett	83 Westhampnett
92 Chichester	92 Chichester	83 Chichester	84 Chichester	84 Chichester
93 Midhurst	93 Midhurst	84 Midhurst	85 Midhurst	85 Midhurst
94 Westbourne	94 Westbourne	85 Westbourne	86 Westbourne	86 Westbourne
95 Havant	95 Havant	86 Havant	87 Havant	87 Havant
96 Portsea Island	96 Portsea Island	87 Portsea Island	88 Portsea Island	88 Portsea Island
97 Alverstoke	97 Alverstoke	88 Alverstoke	89 Alverstoke	89 Alverstoke
98 Fareham	98 Fareham	89 Fareham	90 Fareham	90 Fareham
99 Isle of Wight	99 Isle of Wight	90 Isle of Wight	91 Isle of Wight	91 Isle of Wight
100 Lymington	100 Lymington	91 Lymington	92 Lymington	92 Lymington
101 Christchurch	101 Christchurch	92 Christchurch	93 Christchurch	93 Christchurch
102 Ringwood	102 Ringwood	93 Ringwood	94 Ringwood	94 Ringwood
103 Fordingbridge	103 Fordingbridge	94 Fordingbridge	95 Fordingbridge	95 Fordingbridge
104 New Forest	104 New Forest	95 New Forest	96 New Forest	96 New Forest
105 Southampton	105 Southampton	96 Southampton	97 Southampton	97 Southampton
106 South Stoneham	106 South Stoneham	97 South Stoneham	98 South Stoneham	98 South Stoneham

District	1851	1861	1871	1881	1891	County
Romsey	107	107	98	99	99	Hampshire
Stockbridge	108	108	99	100	100	
Winchester	109	109	100	101	101	
Droxford	110	110	101	102	102	
Catherington	111	111	102	103	103	
Petersfield	112	112	103	104	104	
Alresford	113	113	104	105	105	
Alton	114	114	105	106	106	
Hartley Wintney	115	115	106	107	107	
Basingstoke	116	116	107	108	108	
Whitchurch	117	117	108	109	109	
Andover	118	118	109	110	110	
Kingsclere	119	119	110	111	111	
Newbury	120	120	111	112	112	Berkshire
Hungerford	121	121	112	113	113	
Faringdon	122	122	113	114	114	
Abingdon	123	123	114	115	115	
Wantage	124	124	115	116	116	
Wallingford	125	125	116	117	117	
Bradfield	126	126	117	118	118	
Reading	127	127	118	119	119	
Wokingham	128	128	119	120	120	
Cookham	129	129	120	121	121	
Easthampstead	130	130	121	122	122	
Windsor	131	131	122	123	123	
Staines	132	132	123	124	124	Middlesex
Uxbridge	133	133	124	125	125	
Brentford	134	134	125	126	126	

1851	1861	1871	1881	1891	County
135 Hendon	135 Hendon	126 Hendon	127 Hendon	127 Hendon	
136 Barnet	136 Barnet	127 Barnet	128 Barnet	128 Barnet	
137 Edmonton	137 Edmonton	128 Edmonton	129 Edmonton	129 Edmonton	Middlesex
138 Ware	138 Ware	129 Ware	130 Ware	130 Ware	
139 Bishops Stortford	139 Bishops Stortford	130 Bishops Stortford	131 Bishops Stortford	131 Bishops Stortford	
140 Royston	140 Royston	131 Royston	132 Royston	132 Royston	
141 Hitchin	141 Hitchin	132 Hitchin	133 Hitchin	133 Hitchin	
142 Hertford	142 Hertford	133 Hertford	134 Hertford	134 Hertford	
143 Hatfield	143 Hatfield	134 Hatfield	135 Hatfield	135 Hatfield	
144 St Albans	144 St Albans	135 St Albans	136 St Albans	136 St Albans	
145 Watford	145 Watford	136 Watford	137 Watford	137 Watford	
146 Hemel Hempstead	146 Hemel Hempstead	137 Hemel Hempstead	138 Hemel Hempstead	138 Hemel Hempstead	
147 Berkhamsted	147 Berkhamsted	138 Berkhamsted	139 Berkhamsted	139 Berkhamsted	Hertfordshire
148 Amersham	148 Amersham	139 Amersham	140 Amersham	140 Amersham	
149 Eton	149 Eton	140 Eton	141 Eton	141 Eton	
150 Wycombe	150 Wycombe	141 Wycombe	142 Wycombe	142 Wycombe	
151 Aylesbury	151 Aylesbury	142 Aylesbury	143 Aylesbury	143 Aylesbury	
152 Winslow	152 Winslow	143 Winslow	144 Winslow	144 Winslow	
153 Newport Pagnell	153 Newport Pagnell	144 Newport Pagnell	145 Newport Pagnell	145 Newport Pagnell	
154 Buckingham	154 Buckingham	145 Buckingham	146 Buckingham	146 Buckingham	Buckinghamshire
155 Henley	155 Henley	146 Henley	147 Henley	147 Henley	
156 Thame	156 Thame	147 Thame	148 Thame	148 Thame	
157 Headington	157 Headington	148 Headington	149 Headington	149 Headington	
158 Oxford	158 Oxford	149 Oxford	150 Oxford	150 Oxford	
159 Bicester	159 Bicester	150 Bicester	151 Bicester	151 Bicester	
160 Woodstock	160 Woodstock	151 Woodstock	152 Woodstock	152 Woodstock	
161 Witney	161 Witney	152 Witney	153 Witney	153 Witney	
162 Chipping Norton	162 Chipping Norton	153 Chipping Norton	154 Chipping Norton	154 Chipping Norton	

1851	1861	1871	1881	1891	District	County
163	163	154	155	155	Banbury	Oxfordshire
164	164	155	156	156	Brackley	Northamptonshire
165	165	156	157	157	Towcester	
166	166	157	158	158	Potterspury	
167	167	158	159	159	Hardingstone	
168	168	159	160	160	Northampton	
169	169	160	161	161	Daventry	
170	170	161	162	162	Brixworth	
171	171	162	163	163	Wellingborough	
172	172	163	164	164	Kettering	
173	173	164	165	165	Thrapston	
174	174	165	166	166	Oundle	
175	175	166	167	167	Peterborough	
176	176	167	168	168	Huntingdon	Huntingdonshire
177	177	168	169	169	St Ives	
178	178	169	170	170	St Neots	
179	179	170	171	171	Bedford	Bedfordshire
180	180	171	172	172	Biggleswade	
181	181	172	173	173	Ampthill	
182	182	173	174	174	Woburn	
183	183	174	175	175	Leighton Buzzard	
184	184	175	176	176	Luton	
185	185	176	177	177	Caxton	Cambridgeshire
186	186	177	178	178	Chesterton	
187	187	178	179	179	Cambridge	
188	188	179	180	180	Linton	
189	189	180	181	181	Newmarket	
190	190	181	182	182	Ely	

	1851	1861	1871	1881	1891	County
North Witchford	191	191	182	183	183	Cambridgeshire
Whittlesey	192	192	183	184	184	
Wisbech	193	193	184	185	185	
West Ham	194	194	185	186	186	Essex
Epping	195	195	186	187	187	
Ongar	196	196	187	188	188	
Romford	197	197	188	189	189	
Orsett	198	198	189	190	190	
Billericay	199	199	190	191	191	
Chelmsford	200	200	191	192	192	
Rochford	201	201	192	193	193	
Maldon	202	202	193	194	194	
Tendring	203	203	194	195	195	
Colchester	204	204	195	196	196	
Lexden	205	205	196	197	197	
Witham	206	206	197	pt Lexden	pt Lexden	
Halstead	207	207	198	198	198	
Braintree	208	208	199	199	199	
Dunmow	209	209	200	200	200	
Saffron Walden	210	210	201	201	201	
Risbridge	211	211	202	202	202	
Sudbury	212	212	203	203	203	
Cosford	213	213	204	204	204	
Thingoe	214	214	205	205	205	
Bury St Edmunds	215	215	206	206	206	
Mildenhall	216	216	207	207	207	
Stow	217	217	208	208	208	
Hartismere	218	218	209	209	209	

Suffolk

1851		1861		1871		1881		1891	
219	Hoxne	219	Hoxne	210	Hoxne	210	Hoxne	210	Hoxne
220	Bosmere	220	Bosmere	211	Bosmere	211	Bosmere	211	Bosmere
221	Samford	221	Samford	212	Samford	212	Samford	212	Samford
222	Ipswich	222	Ipswich	213	Ipswich	213	Ipswich	213	Ipswich
223	Woodbridge	223	Woodbridge	214	Woodbridge	214	Woodbridge	214	Woodbridge
224	Plomesgate	224	Plomesgate	215	Plomesgate	215	Plomesgate	215	Plomesgate
225	Blything	225	Blything	216	Blything	216	Blything	216	Blything
226	Wangford	226	Wangford	217	Wangford	217	Wangford	217	Wangford
227	Mutford	227	Mutford	218	Mutford	218	Mutford	218	Mutford
228	Yarmouth	228	Yarmouth	219	Yarmouth	219	Yarmouth	219	Yarmouth
229	Flegg	229	Flegg	220	Flegg	220	Flegg	220	Flegg
230	Tunstead	230	Tunstead	221	Smallburgh	221	Smallburgh	221	Smallburgh
231	Erpingham	231	Erpingham	222	Erpingham	222	Erpingham	222	Erpingham
232	Aylsham	232	Aylsham	223	Aylsham	223	Aylsham	223	Aylsham
233	St Faith's	233	St Faith's	224	St Faith's	224	St Faith's	224	St Faith's
234	Norwich	234	Norwich	225	Norwich	225	Norwich	225	Norwich
235	Forehoe	235	Forehoe	226	Forehoe	226	Forehoe	226	Forehoe
236	Henstead	236	Henstead	227	Henstead	227	Henstead	227	Henstead
237	Blofield	237	Blofield	228	Blofield	228	Blofield	228	Blofield
238	Loddon	238	Loddon	229	Loddon	229	Loddon	229	Loddon
239	Depwade	239	Depwade	230	Depwade	230	Depwade	230	Depwade
240	Guiltcross	240	Guiltcross	231	Guiltcross	231	Guiltcross	231	Guiltcross
241	Wayland	241	Wayland	232	Wayland	232	Wayland	232	Wayland
242	Mitford	242	Mitford	233	Mitford	233	Mitford	233	Mitford
243	Walsingham	243	Walsingham	234	Walsingham	234	Walsingham	234	Walsingham
244	Docking	244	Docking	235	Docking	235	Docking	235	Docking
245	Freebridge Lynn	245	Freebridge Lynn	236	Freebridge Lynn	236	Freebridge Lynn	236	Freebridge Lynn
246	King's Lynn	246	King's Lynn	237	King's Lynn	237	King's Lynn	237	King's Lynn

Norfolk

Norfolk / Wiltshire

1851	1861	1871	1881	1891
247 Downham	247 Downham	238 Downham	238 Downham	238 Downham
248 Swaffham	248 Swaffham	239 Swaffham	239 Swaffham	239 Swaffham
249 Thetford	249 Thetford	240 Thetford	240 Thetford	240 Thetford
250 Highworth	250 Highworth	241 Highworth	241 Highworth	241 Highworth
251 Cricklade	251 Cricklade	242 Cricklade	242 Cricklade	242 Cricklade
252 Malmesbury	252 Malmesbury	243 Malmesbury	243 Malmesbury	243 Malmesbury
253 Chippenham	253 Chippenham	244 Chippenham	244 Chippenham	244 Chippenham
254 Calne	254 Calne	245 Calne	245 Calne	245 Calne
255 Marlborough	255 Marlborough	246 Marlborough	246 Marlborough	246 Marlborough
256 Devizes	256 Devizes	247 Devizes	247 Devizes	247 Devizes
257 Melksham	257 Melksham	248 Melksham	248 Melksham	248 Melksham
258 Bradford on Avon	258 Bradford on Avon	249 Bradford on Avon	249 Bradford on Avon	249 Bradford on Avon
259 Westbury	259 Westbury	250 Westbury	250 Westbury	250 Westbury
260 Warminster	260 Warminster	251 Warminster	251 Warminster	251 Warminster
261 Pewsey	261 Pewsey	252 Pewsey	252 Pewsey	252 Pewsey
262 Amesbury	262 Amesbury	253 Amesbury	253 Amesbury	253 Amesbury
263 Alderbury	263 Alderbury	254 Alderbury	254 Alderbury	254 Alderbury
264 Salisbury	264 Salisbury	pt Alderbury	pt Alderbury	pt Alderbury
265 Wilton	265 Wilton	255 Wilton	255 Wilton	255 Wilton
266 Tisbury	266 Tisbury	256 Tisbury	256 Tisbury	256 Tisbury
267 Mere	267 Mere	257 Mere	257 Mere	257 Mere
268 Shaftesbury	268 Shaftesbury	258 Shaftesbury	258 Shaftesbury	258 Shaftesbury
269 Sturminster	269 Sturminster	259 Sturminster	259 Sturminster	259 Sturminster
270 Blandford	270 Blandford	260 Blandford	260 Blandford	260 Blandford
271 Wimborne	271 Wimborne	261 Wimborne	261 Wimborne	261 Wimborne
272 Poole	272 Poole	262 Poole	262 Poole	262 Poole
273 Wareham	273 Wareham	263 Wareham	263 Wareham	263 Wareham
274 Weymouth	274 Weymouth	264 Weymouth	264 Weymouth	264 Weymouth

1851		1861		1871		1881		1891	
275	Dorchester	275	Dorchester	265	Dorchester	265	Dorchester	265	Dorchester
276	Sherborne	276	Sherborne	266	Sherborne	266	Sherborne	266	Sherborne
277	Beaminster	277	Beaminster	267	Beaminster	267	Beaminster	267	Beaminster
278	Bridport	278	Bridport	268	Bridport	268	Bridport	268	Bridport
279	Axminster	279	Axminster	269	Axminster	269	Axminster	269	Axminster
280	Honiton	280	Honiton	270	Honiton	270	Honiton	270	Honiton
281	St Thomas	281	St Thomas	271	St Thomas	271	St Thomas	271	St Thomas
282	Exeter	282	Exeter	272	Exeter	272	Exeter	272	Exeter
283	Newton Abbot	283	Newton Abbot	273	Newton Abbot	273	Newton Abbot	273	Newton Abbot
284	Totnes	284	Totnes	274	Totnes	274	Totnes	274	Totnes
285	Kingsbridge	285	Kingsbridge	275	Kingsbridge	275	Kingsbridge	275	Kingsbridge
286	Plympton St Mary	286	Plympton St Mary	276	Plympton St Mary	276	Plympton St Mary	276	Plympton St Mary
287	Plymouth	287	Plymouth	277	Plymouth	277	Plymouth	277	Plymouth
288	East Stonehouse	288	East Stonehouse	278	East Stonehouse	278	East Stonehouse	278	East Stonehouse
289	Stoke Damerel	289	Stoke Damerel	279	Stoke Damerel	279	Stoke Damerel	279	Stoke Damerel
290	Tavistock	290	Tavistock	280	Tavistock	280	Tavistock	280	Tavistock
291	Okehampton	291	Okehampton	281	Okehampton	281	Okehampton	281	Okehampton
292	Crediton	292	Crediton	282	Crediton	282	Crediton	282	Crediton
293	Tiverton	293	Tiverton	283	Tiverton	283	Tiverton	283	Tiverton
294	South Molton	294	South Molton	284	South Molton	284	South Molton	284	South Molton
295	Barnstaple	295	Barnstaple	285	Barnstaple	285	Barnstaple	285	Barnstaple
296	Torrington	296	Torrington	286	Torrington	286	Torrington	286	Torrington
297	Bideford	297	Bideford	287	Bideford	287	Bideford	287	Bideford
298	Holsworthy	298	Holsworthy	288	Holsworthy	288	Holsworthy	288	Holsworthy
299	Stratton	299	Stratton	289	Stratton	289	Stratton	289	Stratton
300	Camelford	300	Camelford	290	Camelford	290	Camelford	290	Camelford
301	Launceston	301	Launceston	291	Launceston	291	Launceston	291	Launceston
302	St Germans	302	St Germans	292	St Germans	292	St Germans	292	St Germans

Dorset · **Devonshire** · **Cornwall**

	1851		1861		1871		1881		1891	
Cornwall	303	Liskeard	303	Liskeard	293	Liskeard	293	Liskeard	293	Liskeard
	304	Bodmin	304	Bodmin	294	Bodmin	294	Bodmin	294	Bodmin
	305	St Columb	305	St Columb	295	St Columb	295	St Columb	295	St Columb
	306	St Austell	306	St Austell	296	St Austell	296	St Austell	296	St Austell
	307	Truro	307	Truro	297	Truro	297	Truro	297	Truro
	308	Falmouth	308	Falmouth	298	Falmouth	298	Falmouth	298	Falmouth
	309	Helston	309	Helston	299	Helston	299	Helston	299	Helston
	310	Redruth	310	Redruth	300	Redruth	300	Redruth	300	Redruth
	311	Penzance	311	Penzance	301	Penzance	301	Penzance	301	Penzance
	312	Scilly Isles	312	Scilly Isles	302	Scilly Isles	302	Scilly Isles	302	Scilly Isles
Somerset	313	Williton pt Tiverton	313A	Williton	303	Williton	303	Williton	303	Williton
			313B	Dulverton	304	Dulverton	304	Dulverton	304	Dulverton
	314	Wellington	314	Wellington	305	Wellington	305	Wellington	305	Wellington
	315	Taunton	315	Taunton	306	Taunton	306	Taunton	306	Taunton
	316	Bridgwater	316	Bridgwater	307	Bridgwater	307	Bridgwater	307	Bridgwater
	317	Langport	317	Langport	308	Langport	308	Langport	308	Langport
	318	Chard	318	Chard	309	Chard	309	Chard	309	Chard
	319	Yeovil	319	Yeovil	310	Yeovil	310	Yeovil	310	Yeovil
	320	Wincanton	320	Wincanton	311	Wincanton	311	Wincanton	311	Wincanton
	321	Frome	321	Frome	312	Frome	312	Frome	312	Frome
	322	Shepton Mallet	322	Shepton Mallet	313	Shepton Mallet	313	Shepton Mallet	313	Shepton Mallet
	323	Wells	323	Wells	314	Wells	314	Wells	314	Wells
	324	Axbridge	324	Axbridge	315	Axbridge	315	Axbridge	315	Axbridge
	325	Clutton	325	Clutton	316	Clutton	316	Clutton	316	Clutton
	326	Bath	326	Bath	317	Bath	317	Bath	317	Bath
	327	Keynsham	327	Keynsham	318	Keynsham	318	Keynsham	318	Keynsham
	328	Bedminster	328	Bedminster	319	Bedminster	319	Bedminster	319	Bedminster
	329	Bristol	329	Bristol	320	Bristol	320	Bristol	320	Bristol

1851		1861		1871		1881		1891	
330	Clifton	330	Clifton	321	Clifton	321	Barton Regis	321	Barton Regis
331	Chipping Sodbury	331	Chipping Sodbury	322	Chipping Sodbury	322	Chipping Sodbury	322	Chipping Sodbury
332	Thornbury	332	Thornbury	323	Thornbury	323	Thornbury	323	Thornbury
333	Dursley	333	Dursley	324	Dursley	324	Dursley	324	Dursley
334	Westbury on Severn	334	Westbury on Severn	325	Westbury on Severn	325	Westbury on Severn	325	Westbury on Severn
335	Newent	335	Newent	326	Newent	326	Newent	326	Newent
336	Gloucester	336	Gloucester	327	Gloucester	327	Gloucester	327	Gloucester
337	Wheatenhurst	337	Wheatenhurst	328	Wheatenhurst	328	Wheatenhurst	328	Wheatenhurst
338	Stroud	338	Stroud	329	Stroud	329	Stroud	329	Stroud
339	Tetbury	339	Tetbury	330	Tetbury	330	Tetbury	330	Tetbury
340	Cirencester	340	Cirencester	331	Cirencester	331	Cirencester	331	Cirencester
341	Northleach	341	Northleach	332	Northleach	332	Northleach	332	Northleach
342	Stow-on-the-Wold	342	Stow on the Wold	333	Stow on the Wold	333	Stow on the Wold	333	Stow on the Wold
343	Winchcomb	343	Winchcomb	334	Winchcomb	334	Winchcomb	334	Winchcomb
344	Cheltenham	344	Cheltenham	335	Cheltenham	335	Cheltenham	335	Cheltenham
345	Tewkesbury	345	Tewkesbury	336	Tewkesbury	336	Tewkesbury	336	Tewkesbury **Gloucestershire**
346	Ledbury	346	Ledbury	337	Ledbury	337	Ledbury	337	Ledbury
347	Ross	347	Ross	338	Ross	338	Ross	338	Ross
348	Hereford	348	Hereford	339	Hereford	339	Hereford	339	Hereford
349	Weobly	349	Weobley	340	Weobley	340	Weobley	340	Weobley
350	Bromyard	350	Bromyard	341	Bromyard	341	Bromyard	341	Bromyard
351	Leominster pt Presteigne	351	Leominster pt Presteigne	342	Leominster	342	Leominster	342	Leominster
				343	Kington	343	Kington	343	Kington **Herefordshire**
352	Ludlow	352	Ludlow	344	Ludlow	344	Ludlow	344	Ludlow
353	Clun	353	Clun	345	Clun	345	Clun	345	Clun
354	Church Stretton	354	Church Stretton	346	Church Stretton	346	Church Stretton	346	Church Stretton
355	Cleobury Mortimer	355	Cleobury Mortimer	347	Cleobury Mortimer	347	Cleobury Mortimer	347	Cleobury Mortimer
356	Bridgnorth	356	Bridgnorth	348	Bridgnorth	348	Bridgnorth	348	Bridgnorth **Shropshire**

1851	1861	1871	1881	1891	
357 Shifnal	357 Shifnal	349 Shifnal	349 Shifnal	349 Shifnal	
358 Madeley	358 Madeley	350 Madeley	350 Madeley	350 Madeley	
359 Atcham	359 Atcham	351 Atcham	351 Atcham	351 Atcham	
360 Shrewsbury	360 Shrewsbury	352 Shrewsbury	pt Atcham	pt Atcham	
361 Oswestry	361 Oswestry	353 Oswestry	352 Oswestry	352 Oswestry	
362 Ellesmere	362 Ellesmere	354 Ellesmere	353 Ellesmere	353 Ellesmere	
363 Wem	363A Wem	355 Wem	354 Wem	354 Wem	
pt Wem	363B Whitchurch	356 Whitchurch	355 Whitchurch	355 Whitchurch	
364 Market Drayton	364 Market Drayton	357 Market Drayton	356 Market Drayton	356 Market Drayton	
365 Wellington	365 Wellington	358 Wellington	357 Wellington	357 Wellington	
366 Newport	366 Newport	359 Newport	358 Newport	358 Newport	**Shropshire**
367 Stafford	367 Stafford	360 Stafford	359 Stafford	359 Stafford	
368 Stone	368 Stone	361 Stone	360 Stone	360 Stone	
369 Newcastle under Lyme	369 Newcastle under Lyme	362 Newcastle under Lyme	361 Newcastle under Lyme	361 Newcastle under Lyme	
370 Wolstanton	370 Wolstanton	363 Wolstanton	362 Wolstanton	362 Wolstanton	
371 Stoke on Trent	371 Stoke on Trent	364 Stoke on Trent	363 Stoke on Trent	363 Stoke on Trent	
372 Leek	372 Leek	365 Leek	364 Leek	364 Leek	
373 Cheadle	373 Cheadle	366 Cheadle	365 Cheadle	365 Cheadle	
374 Uttoxeter	374 Uttoxeter	367 Uttoxeter	366 Uttoxeter	366 Uttoxeter	
375 Burton upon Trent	375 Burton upon Trent	368 Burton upon Trent	367 Burton upon Trent	367 Burton-upon-Trent	
376 Tamworth	376 Tamworth	369 Tamworth	368 Tamworth	368 Tamworth	
377 Lichfield	377 Lichfield	370 Lichfield	369 Lichfield	369 Lichfield	
378 Penkridge	378 Penkridge	371 Penkridge	370 Cannock	370 Cannock	
379 Wolverhampton	379 Wolverhampton	372 Wolverhampton	371 Wolverhampton	371 Wolverhampton	
380 Walsall	380 Walsall	373 Walsall	372 Walsall	372 Walsall	
381 West Bromwich	381 West Bromwich	374 West Bromwich	373 West Bromwich	373 West Bromwich	
382 Dudley	382 Dudley	375 Dudley	374 Dudley	374 Dudley	**Staffordshire**
383 Stourbridge	383 Stourbridge	376 Stourbridge	375 Stourbridge	375 Stourbridge	

1851		1861		1871		1881		1891		County
384	Kidderminster	384	Kidderminster	377	Kidderminster	376	Kidderminster	376	Kidderminster	
385	Tenbury	385	Tenbury	378	Tenbury	377	Tenbury	377	Tenbury	
386	Martley	386	Martley	379	Martley	378	Martley	378	Martley	
387	Worcester	387	Worcester	380	Worcester	379	Worcester	379	Worcester	
388	Upton on Severn	388	Upton on Severn	381	Upton on Severn	380	Upton on Severn	380	Upton on Severn	
389	Evesham	389	Evesham	382	Evesham	381	Evesham	381	Evesham	
390	Pershore	390	Pershore	383	Pershore	382	Pershore	382	Pershore	
391	Droitwich	391	Droitwich	384	Droitwich	383	Droitwich	383	Droitwich	
392	Bromsgrove	392	Bromsgrove	385	Bromsgrove	384	Bromsgrove	384	Bromsgrove	
393	King's Norton	393	King's Norton	386	King's Norton	385	King's Norton	385	King's Norton	Worcestershire
394	Birmingham	394	Birmingham	387	Birmingham	386	Birmingham	386	Birmingham	
395	Aston	395	Aston	388	Aston	387	Aston	387	Aston	
396	Meriden	396	Meriden	389	Meriden	388	Meriden	388	Meriden	
397	Atherstone	397	Atherstone	390	Atherstone	389	Atherstone	389	Atherstone	
398	Nuneaton	398	Nuneaton	391	Nuneaton	390	Nuneaton	390	Nuneaton	
399	Foleshill	399	Foleshill	392	Foleshill	391	Foleshill	391	Foleshill	
400	Coventry	400	Coventry	393	Coventry	392	Coventry	392	Coventry	
401	Rugby	401	Rugby	394	Rugby	393	Rugby	393	Rugby	
402	Solihull	402	Solihull	395	Solihull	394	Solihull	394	Solihull	
403	Warwick	403	Warwick	396	Warwick	395	Warwick	395	Warwick	
404	Stratford on Avon	404	Stratford on Avon	397	Stratford on Avon	396	Stratford on Avon	396	Stratford on Avon	
405	Alcester	405	Alcester	398	Alcester	397	Alcester	397	Alcester	
406	Shipston on Stour	406	Shipston on Stour	399	Shipston on Stour	398	Shipston on Stour	398	Shipston on Stour	
407	Southam	407	Southam	400	Southam	399	Southam	399	Southam	Warwickshire
408	Lutterworth	408	Lutterworth	401	Lutterworth	400	Lutterworth	400	Lutterworth	
409	Market Harborough	409	Market Harborough	402	Market Harborough	401	Market Harborough	401	Market Harborough	
410	Billesdon	410	Billesdon	403	Billesdon	402	Billesdon	402	Billesdon	
411	Blaby	411	Blaby	404	Blaby	403	Blaby	403	Blaby	Leicestershire

	1851	1861	1871	1881	1891
Hinckley	412	412	405	404	404
Market Bosworth	413	413	406	405	405
Ashby de la Zouch	414	414	407	406	406
Loughborough	415	415	408	407	407
Barrow on Soar	416	416	409	408	408
Leicester	417	417	410	409	409
Melton Mowbray *(Leicestershire)*	418	418	411	410	410
Oakham	419	419	412	411	411
Uppingham *(Rutland)*	420	420	413	412	412
Stamford	421	421	414	413	413
Bourne	422	422	415	414	414
Spalding	423	423	416	415	415
Holbeach	424	424	417	416	416
Boston	425	425	418	417	417
Sleaford	426	426	419	418	418
Grantham	427	427	420	419	419
Lincoln	428	428	421	420	420
Horncastle	429	429	422	421	421
Spilsby	430	430	423	422	422
Louth	431	431	424	423	423
Caistor	432	432	425	424	424
Glanford Brigg	433	433	426	425	425
Gainsborough *(Lincolnshire)*	434	434	427	426	426
East Retford	435	435	428	427	427
Worksop	436	436	429	428	428
Mansfield	437	437	430	429	429
Basford	438	438	431	430	430
Radford	439	439	432		
pt Nottingham				pt Nottingham	pt Nottingham

District	1851	1861	1871	1881	1891
Nottinghamshire					
Nottingham	440	440	433	431	431
Southwell	441	441	434	432	432
Newark	442	442	435	433	433
Bingham	443	443	436	434	434
Derbyshire					
Shardlow	444	444	437	435	435
Derby	445	445	438	436	436
Belper	446	446	439	437	437
Ashbourne	447	447	440	438	438
Chesterfield	448	448	441	439	439
Bakewell	449	449	442	440	440
Chapel en le Frith	450	450	443	441	441
Hayfield	451	451	444	442	442
Cheshire					
Stockport	452	452	445	443	443
Macclesfield	453	453	446	444	444
Altrincham	454	454	447	445	445
Runcorn	455	455	448	446	446
Northwich	456	456	449	447	447
Congleton	457	457	450	448	448
Nantwich	458	458	451	449	449
Great Boughton / Chester	459 (Great Boughton)	459 (Great Boughton)	452 (Chester)	450 (Chester)	450 (Chester)
Wirral	460	460A	453	451	451
pt Wirral	pt Wirral				
Birkenhead	460B	460B	454	452	452
Lancashire					
Liverpool	461	461	455	453	453
pt Liverpool	pt Liverpool	pt Liverpool	pt Liverpool		
Toxteth Park					454
West Derby	462	462	456	455	455
Prescot	463	463	457	456	456
Ormskirk	464	464	458	457	457
Wigan	465	465	459	458	458

1851	1861	1871	1881	1891 Lancashire
466 Warrington	466 Warrington	460 Warrington	459 Warrington	459 Warrington
467 Leigh	467 Leigh	461 Leigh	460 Leigh	460 Leigh
468 Bolton	468 Bolton	462 Bolton	461 Bolton	461 Bolton
469 Bury	469 Bury	463 Bury	462 Bury	462 Bury
470 Barton upon Irwell	470 Barton upon Irwell	464 Barton upon Irwell	463 Barton upon Irwell	463 Barton upon Irwell
471 Chorlton	471 Chorlton	465 Chorlton	464 Chorlton	464 Chorlton
472 Salford	472 Salford	466 Salford	465 Salford	465 Salford
473 Manchester	473 Manchester	467 Manchester	466 Manchester	466 Manchester
pt Manchester	pt Manchester	pt Manchester	467 Prestwich	467 Prestwich
474 Ashton under Lyne	474 Ashton under Lyne	468 Ashton under Lyne	468 Ashton under Lyne	468 Ashton under Lyne
475 Oldham	475 Oldham	469 Oldham	469 Oldham	469 Oldham
476 Rochdale	476 Rochdale	470 Rochdale	470 Rochdale	470 Rochdale
477 Haslingden	477 Haslingden	471 Haslingden	471 Haslingden	471 Haslingden
478 Burnley	478 Burnley	472 Burnley	472 Burnley	472 Burnley
479 Clitheroe	479 Clitheroe	473 Clitheroe	473 Clitheroe	473 Clitheroe
480 Blackburn	480 Blackburn	474 Blackburn	474 Blackburn	474 Blackburn
481 Chorley	481 Chorley	475 Chorley	475 Chorley	475 Chorley
482 Preston	482 Preston	476 Preston	476 Preston	476 Preston
483 Fylde	483 Fylde	477 Fylde	477 Fylde	477 Fylde
484 Garstang	484 Garstang	478 Garstang	478 Garstang	478 Garstang
485 Lancaster	485 Lancaster	479 Lancaster	479 Lancaster	479 Lancaster
pt Lancaster	pt Lancaster	480 Lunesdale	480 Lunesdale	480 Lunesdale
486 Ulverston	486 Ulverston	481 Ulverston	481 Ulverston	481 Ulverston
pt Ulverston	pt Ulverston	pt Ulverston	482 Barrow in Furness	482 Barrow in Furness
487 Sedbergh	487 Sedbergh	482 Sedbergh	483 Sedburgh	483 Sedburgh
488 Settle	488 Settle	483 Settle	484 Settle	484 Settle
489 Skipton	489 Skipton	484 Skipton	485 Skipton	485 Skipton
490 Pateley Bridge	490 Pateley Bridge	485 Pateley Bridge	486 Pateley Bridge	486 Pateley Bridge

W. Riding Yorkshire

1851	1861	1871	1881	1891
491 Ripon	491 Ripon	486 Ripon	487 Ripon	487 Ripon
pt Knaresborough				
	492A Great Ouseburn	487 Great Ouseburn	488 Great Ouseburn	488 Great Ouseburn
492 Knaresborough	492B Knaresborough	488 Knaresborough	489 Knaresborough	489 Knaresborough
pt Knaresborough	492C Wetherby	489 Wetherby	490 Wetherby	490 Wetherby
pt Knaresborough	492D Kirk Deighton	pt Wetherby	pt Wetherby	pt Wetherby
		pt Wharfedale	pt Wharfedale	pt Wharfedale
493 Otley	493A Otley			
pt Otley	493B Wharfedale	490 Wharfedale	491 Wharfedale	491 Wharfedale
494 Keighley	494 Keighley	491 Keighley	492 Keighley	492 Keighley
495 Todmorden	495 Todmorden	492 Todmorden	493 Todmorden	493 Todmorden
496 Saddleworth	496 Saddleworth	493 Saddleworth	494 Saddleworth	494 Saddleworth
497 Huddersfield	497 Huddersfield	494 Huddersfield	495 Huddersfield	495 Huddersfield
498 Halifax	498 Halifax	495 Halifax	496 Halifax	496 Halifax
499 Bradford	499 Bradford	496 Bradford	497 Bradford	497 Bradford
500 Hunslet	500 Hunslet	497 Hunslet	498 Hunslet	498 Hunslet
pt Hunslet	pt Hunslet	498 Holbeck	499 Holbeck	499 Holbeck
pt Hunslet	pt Hunslet	499 Bramley	500 Bramley	500 Bramley
501 Leeds	501 Leeds	500 Leeds	501 Leeds	501 Leeds
502 Dewsbury	502 Dewsbury	501 Dewsbury	502 Dewsbury	502 Dewsbury
503 Wakefield	503 Wakefield	502 Wakefield	503 Wakefield	503 Wakefield
504 Pontefract	504A Pontefract	503 Pontefract	504 Pontefract	504 Pontefract
pt Pontefract	504B Hemsworth	504 Hemsworth	505 Hemsworth	505 Hemsworth
505 Barnsley	505 Barnsley	505 Barnsley	506 Barnsley	506 Barnsley
506 Wortley	506 Wortley	506 Wortley	507 Wortley	507 Wortley
507 Ecclesall Bierlow	507 Ecclesall Bierlow	507 Ecclesall Bierlow	508 Ecclesall Bierlow	508 Ecclesall Bierlow
508 Sheffield	508 Sheffield	508 Sheffield	509 Sheffield	509 Sheffield
509 Rotherham	509 Rotherham	509 Rotherham	510 Rotherham	510 Rotherham
510 Doncaster	510 Doncaster	510 Doncaster	511 Doncaster	511 Doncaster
511 Thorne	511 Thorne	511 Thorne	512 Thorne	512 Thorne

1851	1861	1871	1881	1891	Riding
512 Goole	512 Goole	512 Goole	513 Goole	513 Goole	**W. Riding Yorkshire**
513 Selby	513 Selby	513 Selby	514 Selby	514 Selby	
514 Tadcaster	514 Tadcaster	514 Tadcaster	515 Tadcaster	515 Tadcaster	
515 York	515 York	515 York	516 York	516 York	
516 Pocklington	516 Pocklington	516 Pocklington	517 Pocklington	517 Pocklington	
517 Howden	517 Howden	517 Howden	518 Howden	518 Howden	
518 Beverley	518 Beverley	518 Beverley	519 Beverley	519 Beverley	
519 Sculcoates	519 Sculcoates	519 Sculcoates	520 Sculcoates	520 Sculcoates	
520 Hull	520 Hull	520 Hull	521 Hull	521 Hull	
521 Patrington	521 Patrington	521 Patrington	522 Patrington	522 Patrington	
522 Skirlaugh	522 Skirlaugh	522 Skirlaugh	523 Skirlaugh	523 Skirlaugh	
523 Driffield	523 Driffield	523 Driffield	524 Driffield	524 Driffield	**E. Riding Yorkshire**
524 Bridlington	524 Bridlington	524 Bridlington	525 Bridlington	525 Bridlington	
525 Scarborough	525 Scarborough	525 Scarborough	526 Scarborough	526 Scarborough	
526 Malton	526 Malton	526 Malton	527 Malton	527 Malton	
527 Easingwold	527 Easingwold	527 Easingwold	528 Easingwold	528 Easingwold	
528 Thirsk	528 Thirsk	528 Thirsk	529 Thirsk	529 Thirsk	
529 Helmsley	529 Helmsley	529 Helmsley	530 Helmsley	530 Helmsley	
530 Pickering	530 Pickering	530 Pickering	531 Pickering	531 Pickering	
531 Whitby	531 Whitby	531 Whitby	532 Whitby	532 Whitby	
532 Guisborough pt Guisborough	532 Guisborough pt Guisborough	532 Guisborough pt Guisborough	533 Guisborough	533 Guisborough	
			534 Middlesbrough	534 Middlesbrough	
533 Stokesley	533 Stokesley	533 Stokesley	535 Stokesley	535 Stokesley	
534 Northallerton	534 Northallerton	534 Northallerton	536 Northallerton	536 Northallerton	
535 Bedale	535 Bedale	535 Bedale	537 Bedale	537 Bedale	
536 Leyburn	536 Leyburn	536 Leyburn	538 Leyburn	538 Leyburn	
537 Askrigg	537 Askrigg	537 Aysgarth	539 Aysgarth	539 Aysgarth	
538 Reeth	538 Reeth	538 Reeth	540 Reeth	540 Reeth	**N. Riding Yorkshire**
539 Richmond	539 Richmond	539 Richmond	541 Richmond	541 Richmond	

1851	1861	1871	1881	1891	County
540 Darlington	540 Darlington	540 Darlington	542 Darlington	542 Darlington	Durham
541 Stockton	541A Stockton	541 Stockton	543 Stockton	543 Stockton	
pt Stockton	541B Hartlepool	542 Hartlepool	544 Hartlepool	544 Hartlepool	
542 Auckland	542 Auckland	543 Auckland	545 Auckland	545 Auckland	
543 Teesdale	543 Teesdale	544 Teesdale	546 Teesdale	546 Teesdale	
544 Weardale	544 Weardale	545 Weardale	547 Weardale	547 Weardale	
pt Weardale	pt Weardale	pt Weardale	548 Lanchester	548 Lanchester	
545 Durham	545 Durham	546 Durham	549 Durham	549 Durham	
546 Easington	546 Easington	547 Easington	550 Easington	550 Easington	
547 Houghton le Spring	547 Houghton le Spring	548 Houghton le Spring	551 Houghton le Spring	551 Houghton le Spring	
548 Chester le Street	548 Chester le Street	549 Chester le Street	552 Chester le Street	552 Chester le Street	
549 Sunderland	549 Sunderland	550 Sunderland	553 Sunderland	553 Sunderland	
550 South Shields	550 South Shields	551 South Shields	554 South Shields	554 South Shields	
551 Gateshead	551 Gateshead	552 Gateshead	555 Gateshead	555 Gateshead	
552 Newcastle upon Tyne	552 Newcastle upon Tyne	553 Newcastle upon Tyne	556 Newcastle upon Tyne	556 Newcastle upon Tyne	Northumberland
553 Tynemouth	553 Tynemouth	554 Tynemouth	557 Tynemouth	557 Tynemouth	
554 Castle Ward	554 Castle Ward	555 Castle Ward	558 Castle Ward	558 Castle Ward	
555 Hexham	555 Hexham	556 Hexham	559 Hexham	559 Hexham	
556 Haltwhistle	556 Haltwhistle	557 Haltwhistle	560 Haltwhistle	560 Haltwhistle	
557 Bellingham	557 Bellingham	558 Bellingham	561 Bellingham	561 Bellingham	
558 Morpeth	558 Morpeth	559 Morpeth	562 Morpeth	562 Morpeth	
559 Alnwick	559 Alnwick	560 Alnwick	563 Alnwick	563 Alnwick	
560 Belford	560 Belford	561 Belford	564 Belford	564 Belford	
561 Berwick	561 Berwick	562 Berwick	565 Berwick	565 Berwick	
562 Glendale	562 Glendale	563 Glendale	566 Glendale	566 Glendale	
563 Rothbury	563 Rothbury	564 Rothbury	567 Rothbury	567 Rothbury	
564 Alston	564 Alston	565 Alston	568 Alston	568 Alston	Cumberland
565 Penrith	565 Penrith	566 Penrith	569 Penrith	569 Penrith	

1851	1861	1871	1881	1891	Place	County
566	566	567	570	570	Brampton	Cumberland
567	567	568	571	571	Longtown	
568	568	569	572	572	Carlisle	
569	569	570	573	573	Wigton	
570	570	571	574	574	Cockermouth	
571	571	572	575	575	Whitehaven	
572	572	573	576	576	Bootle	
573	573	574	577	577	East Ward	Westmoreland
574	574	575	578	578	West Ward	
575	575	576	579	579	Kendal	
576	576	577	580	580	Chepstow	Monmouthshire
577	577	578	581	581	Monmouth	
578	578A	579	582	582	Abergavenny	
pt Abergavenny					pt Abergavenny	
	578B	580	583	583	Bedwellty	
579	579	581	584	584	Pontypool	
580	580	582	585	585	Newport	
581	581	583	586	586	Cardiff	Glamorgan
pt Cardiff	pt Cardiff				pt Cardiff	
		584	587	587	Pontypridd	
582	582	585	588	588	Merthyr Tydfil	
583	583	586	589	589	Bridgend	
584	584	587	590	590	Neath	
pt Neath	pt Neath	pt Neath			pt Neath	
			591	591	Pontardawe	
585	585A	588	592	592	Swansea	
pt Swansea					pt Swansea	
	585B	589	593	593	Gower	
586	586	590	594	594	Llanelly	Carmarthen
587	587	591	595	595	Llandovery	
588	588	592	596	596	Llandilofawr	
589	589	593	597	597	Carmarthen	
590	590	594	598	598	Narberth	Pembroke
591	591	595	599	599	Pembroke	
592	592	596	600	600	Haverfordwest	
593	593	597	601	601	Cardigan	

	1851	1861	1871	1881	1891
Cardiganshire	594 Newcastle in Emlyn	594 Newcastle in Emlyn	598 Newcastle in Emlyn	602 Newcastle in Emlyn	602 Newcastle in Emlyn
	595 Lampeter	595 Lampeter	599 Lampeter	603 Lampeter	603 Lampeter
	596 Aberayron	596 Aberayron	600 Aberayron	604 Aberayron	604 Aberayron
	597 Aberystwyth	597 Aberystwyth	601 Aberystwyth	605 Aberystwyth	605 Aberystwyth
	598 Tregaron	598 Tregaron	602 Tregaron	606 Tregaron	606 Tregaron
Brecon	599 Builth	599 Builth	603 Builth	607 Builth	607 Builth
	600 Brecknock	600 Brecknock	604 Brecknock	608 Brecknock	608 Brecknock
	601 Crickhowell	601 Crickhowell	605 Crickhowell	609 Crickhowell	609 Crickhowell
	602 Hay	602 Hay	606 Hay	610 Hay	610 Hay
Radnorshire	603 Presteigne	603 Presteigne	607 Presteigne	pt Knighton	pt Knighton
	604 Knighton	604 Knighton	608 Knighton	611 Knighton	611 Knighton
	605 Rhayader	605 Rhayader	609 Rhayader	612 Rhayader	612 Rhayader
Montgomery	606 Machynlleth	606 Machynlleth	610 Machynlleth	613 Machynlleth	613 Machynlleth
	607 Newtown	607 Newtown	611 Newtown	614 Newtown	614 Newtown
	608 Montgomery	608 Montgomery	612 Forden	615 Forden	615 Forden
	609 Llanfyllin	609 Llanfyllin	613 Llanfyllin	616 Llanfyllin	616 Llanfyllin
Flintshire	610 Holywell	610 Holywell	614 Holywell	617 Holywell	617 Holywell
Denbighshire	611 Wrexham	611 Wrexham	615 Wrexham	618 Wrexham	618 Wrexham
	612 Ruthin	612 Ruthin	616 Ruthin	619 Ruthin	619 Ruthin
	613 St Asaph	613 St Asaph	617 St Asaph	620 St Asaph	620 St Asaph
	614 Llanrwst	614 Llanrwst	618 Llanrwst	621 Llanrwst	621 Llanrwst
Merioneth	615 Corwen	615 Corwen	619 Corwen	622 Corwen	622 Corwen
	616 Bala	616 Bala	620 Bala	623 Bala	623 Bala
	617 Dolgellau	617 Dolgellau	621 Dolgellau	624 Dolgellau	624 Dolgellau
	618 Ffestiniog	618 Ffestiniog	622 Ffestiniog	625 Ffestiniog	625 Ffestiniog
Caernarfon	619 Pwllheli	619 Pwllheli	623 Pwllheli	626 Pwllheli	626 Pwllheli
	620 Caernarfon	620 Caernarfon	624 Caernarfon	627 Caernarfon	627 Caernarfon
	621 Bangor	621 Bangor	625 Bangor	628 Bangor	628 Bangor
	622 Conway	622 Conway	626 Conway	629 Conway	629 Conway
Anglesey	623 Anglesey	623 Anglesey	627 Anglesey	630 Anglesey	630 Anglesey
	pt Anglesey	pt Anglesey	pt Anglesey	pt Anglesey	631 Holyhead

APPENDIX 6   STREET INDEXES 1841

All London registration districts and

RD No	Place	RD No	Place
582	Aberdare	452	Macclesfield
474	Ashton under Lyne	471	Manchester
394	Aston	582	Merthyr Tydfil
329	Bedminster	474	Middleton
394	Birmingham	552	Newcastle upon Tyne
474	Bolton	553	North Shields
499	Bradford	234	Norwich
328	Bristol	440	Nottingham
469	Bury	475	Oldham
400	Coventry	452	Prestbury
46	Croydon	475	Prestwich
469	Deane	96	Portsmouth
328	Dudley	476	Radcliffe
474	Eccles	476	Rochdale
394	Edgbaston	508	Sheffield
474	Flixton	105	Southampton
550	Gateshead	550	South Fields
498	Halifax	105	South Stoneham
497	Huddersfield	549	Sunderland
520	Hull	462	Toxteth Park
499	Leeds	553	Tynemouth
461	Liverpool	462	West Derby

APPENDIX 7 STREET INDEXES 1851

All London registration districts and

RD No	Place	RD No	Place	RD No	Place
46	Croydon	360	Shrewsbury	481	Chorley
47	Kingston	365	Wellington	482	Preston
54	Medway	367	Stafford	485	Lancaster
57	Tonbridge	371	Stoke on Trent	495	Todmorden
58	Maidstone	379	Wolverhampton	496	Saddleworth
85	Brighton	380	Walsall	497	Huddersfield
92	Chichester	381	West Bromwich	498	Halifax
96	Portsea	382	Dudley	499	Bradford
99	Isle of Wight	383	Stourbridge	500	Hunslet
105	Southampton	384	Kidderminster	501	Leeds
106	South Stoneham	387	Worcester	502	Dewsbury
127	Reading	393	King's Norton	503	Wakefield
134	Brentford	394	Birmingham	506	Wortley
135	Hendon	395	Aston	507	Ecclesall Bierlow
136	Barnet	400	Coventry	508	Sheffield
137	Edmonton	417	Leicester	509	Rotherham
158	Oxford	421	Stamford	515	York
168	Northampton	424	Holbeach	519	Sculcoates
179	Bedford	428	Lincoln	520	Hull
183	Leighton Buzzard	440	Nottingham	531	Whitby
184	Luton	445	Derby	541	Stockton
187	Cambridge	452	Stockport	545	Durham
194	West Ham	453	Macclesfield	549	Sunderland
215	Bury St Edmunds	459	Chester	550	South Shields
222	Ipswich	460A	Wirral	551	Gateshead
228	Yarmouth	460B	Birkenhead	552	Newcastle upon Tyne
234	Norwich	461	Liverpool		
246	King's Lynn	462	West Derby	553	Tynemouth
264	Salisbury	463	Prescot	568	Carlisle
281	St Thomas	465	Wigan	570	Cockermouth
282	Exeter	466	Warrington	578	Abergavenny
287	Plymouth	468	Bolton	580	Newport
288	East Stonehouse	469	Bury	581	Cardiff
289	Stoke Damerel	470	Barton upon Irwell	582	Merthyr Tydfil
316	Bridgwater	471	Chorlton	583	Bridgend
326	Bath	472	Salford	584	Neath
327	Keynsham	473	Manchester	585	Swansea
328	Bedminster	474	Ashton under Lyne	598	Tregaron
329	Bristol	475	Oldham	620	Caernarfon
330	Clifton	476	Rochdale	800	Isle of Man
336	Gloucester	477	Haslingden	900	Jersey
344	Cheltenham	480	Blackburn		

APPENDIX 8 STREET INDEXES 1861 AND 1871

All London registration districts and

1861		1871	
RD No	Place	RD No	Place
46	Croydon	37	Croydon
47	Kingston	38	Kingston
54	Medway	45	Medway
57	Tonbridge	48	Tonbridge
58	Maidstone	49	Maidstone
85	Brighton	76	Brighton
96	Portsea	87	Portsea
105	Southampton	96	Southampton
106	South Stoneham	97	South Stoneham
127	Reading	118	Reading
134	Brentford	125	Brentford
135	Hendon	126	Hendon
137	Edmonton	128	Edmonton
158	Oxford	149	Oxford
168	Northampton	159	Northampton
187	Cambridge	178	Cambridge
194	West Ham	185	West Ham
222	Ipswich	213	Ipswich
228	Yarmouth	219	Yarmouth
234	Norwich	225	Norwich
282	Exeter	272	Exeter
287	Plymouth	277	Plymouth
288	East Stonehouse	278	East Stonehouse
289	Stoke Damerel	279	Stoke Damerel
326	Bath	317	Bath
327	Keynsham	318	Keynsham
328	Bedminster	319	Bedminster
329	Bristol	320	Bristol
330	Clifton	321	Clifton
336	Gloucester	327	Gloucester
344	Cheltenham	335	Cheltenham
371	Stoke on Trent	364	Stoke on Trent
379	Wolverhampton	372	Wolverhampton
381	West Bromwich	374	West Bromwich
382	Dudley	375	Dudley

1861		1871	
RD No	Place	RD No	Place
383	Stourbridge	376	Stourbridge
387	Worcester	380	Worcester
393	King's Norton	386	King's Norton
394	Birmingham	387	Birmingham
395	Aston	388	Aston
400	Coventry	393	Coventry
417	Leicester	410	Leicester
440	Nottingham	433	Nottingham
445	Derby	438	Derby
452	Stockport	445	Stockport
453	Macclesfield	446	Macclesfield
459	Chester	452	Chester
460A	Wirral	453	Wirral
460B	Birkenhead	454	Birkenhead
461	Liverpool	455	Liverpool
462	West Derby	456	West Derby
465	Wigan	459	Wigan
468	Bolton	462	Bolton
469	Bury	463	Bury
470	Barton upon Irwell	464	Barton upon Irwell
471	Chorlton	465	Chorlton
472	Salford	466	Salford
473	Manchester	467	Manchester
474	Ashton under Lyne	468	Ashton under Lyne
475	Oldham	469	Oldham
476	Rochdale	470	Rochdale
477	Haslingden	471	Haslingden
480	Blackburn	474	Blackburn
481	Chorley	475	Chorley
482	Preston	476	Preston
485	Lancaster	479	Lancaster
495	Todmorden	492	Todmorden
496	Saddleworth	493	Saddleworth
497	Huddersfield	494	Huddersfield
498	Halifax	495	Halifax
499	Bradford	496	Bradford

1861		1871	
RD No	Place	RD No	Place
500	Hunslet	597	Hunslet
	pt Hunslet	498	Holbeck
	pt Hunslet	499	Bramley
501	Leeds	500	Leeds
506	Wortley	506	Wortley
507	Ecclesall Bierlow	507	Ecclesall Bierlow
508	Sheffield	508	Sheffield
509	Rotherham	509	Rotherham
515	York	515	York
519	Sculcoates	519	Sculcoates
520	Hull	520	Hull
541A	Stockton	541	Stockton
549	Sunderland	550	Sunderland
550	South Shields	551	South Shields
551	Gateshead	552	Gateshead
552	Newcastle upon Tyne	553	Newcastle upon Tyne
553	Tynemouth	554	Tynemouth
568	Carlisle	569	Carlisle
580	Newport	582	Newport
581	Cardiff	583	Cardiff
582	Merthyr Tydfil	585	Merthyr Tydfil
585A	Swansea	588	Swansea
900	Jersey	900	Jersey

APPENDIX 9 STREET INDEXES 1881 AND 1891

All London registration districts and

1881		1891	
RD No	Place	RD No	Place
30	Epsom	30	Epsom
32	Guildford	32	Guildford
33	Farnham	33	Farnham
38	Croydon	38	Croydon
39	Kingston	39	Kingston
40	Richmond	40	Richmond
41	Bromley	41	Bromley
42	Dartford	42	Dartford
46	Medway	46	Medway
49	Tonbridge	49	Tonbridge
50	Maidstone	50	Maidstone
62	Thanet	62	Thanet
64	Dover	64	Dover
65	Elham	65	Elham
68	Hastings	68	Hastings
70	Eastbourne	70	Eastbourne
77	Brighton	77	Brighton
78	Steyning	78	Steyning
88	Portsea	88	Portsea
91	Isle of Wight	91	Isle of Wight
93	Christchurch	93	Christchurch
97	Southampton	97	Southampton
98	South Stoneham	98	South Stoneham
119	Reading	119	Reading
126	Brentford	126	Brentford
127	Hendon	127	Hendon
128	Barnet	128	Barnet
129	Edmonton	129	Edmonton
142	Wycombe	142	Wycombe
149	Headington	149	Headington
150	Oxford	150	Oxford
160	Northampton	160	Northampton

1881		1891	
RD No	Place	RD No	Place
163	Wellingborough	163	Wellingborough
167	Peterborough	167	Peterborough
171	Bedford	171	Bedford
176	Luton	176	Luton
179	Cambridge	179	Cambridge
186	West Ham	186	West Ham
189	Romford	189	Romford
213	Ipswich	213	Ipswich
219	Yarmouth	219	Yarmouth
225	Norwich	225	Norwich
241	Highworth	241	Highworth
271	St Thomas	271	St Thomas
272	Exeter	272	Exeter
273	Newton Abbot	273	Newton Abbot
274	Totnes	274	Totnes
277	Plymouth	277	Plymouth
278	East Stonehouse	278	East Stonehouse
279	Stoke Damerel	279	Stoke Damerel
285	Barnstaple	285	Barnstaple
300	Redruth	300	Redruth
301	Penzance	301	Penzance
315	Axbridge	315	Axbridge
317	Bath	317	Bath
318	Keynsham	318	Keynsham
319	Bedminster	319	Bedminster
320	Bristol	320	Bristol
321	Barton Regis	321	Barton Regis
327	Gloucester	327	Gloucester
329	Stroud	329	Stroud
335	Cheltenham	335	Cheltenham
339	Hereford	339	Hereford
351	Atcham	351	Atcham
362	Wolstanton	362	Wolstanton
363	Stoke on Trent	363	Stoke on Trent
367	Burton upon Trent	367	Burton upon Trent

1881		1891	
RD No.	Place	RD No.	Place
369	Lichfield	369	Lichfield
370	Cannock	370	Cannock
371	Wolverhampton	371	Wolverhampton
372	Walsall	372	Walsall
373	West Bromwich	373	West Bromwich
374	Dudley	374	Dudley
375	Stourbridge	375	Stourbridge
376	Kidderminster	376	Kidderminster
379	Worcester	379	Worcester
385	King's Norton	385	King's Norton
386	Birmingham	386	Birmingham
387	Aston	387	Aston
392	Coventry	392	Coventry
395	Warwick	395	Warwick
409	Leicester	409	Leicester
420	Lincoln	420	Lincoln
424	Caistor	424	Caistor
425	Glanford Brigg	425	Glanford Brigg
429	Mansfield	429	Mansfield
430	Basford	430	Basford
431	Nottingham	431	Nottingham
435	Shardlow	435	Shardlow
436	Derby	436	Derby
437	Belper	437	Belper
439	Chesterfield	439	Chesterfield
443	Stockport	443	Stockport
444	Macclesfield	444	Macclesfield
445	Altrincham	445	Altrincham
446	Runcorn	446	Runcorn
447	Northwich	447	Northwich
449	Nantwich	449	Nantwich
450	Chester	450	Chester
451	Wirral	451	Wirral
452	Birkenhead	452	Birkenhead
453	Liverpool	453	Liverpool

1881		1891	
RD No	Place	RD No	Place
454	Toxteth Park	454	Toxteth Park
455	West Derby	455	West Derby
456	Prescott	456	Prescott
457	Ormskirk	457	Ormskirk
458	Wigan	458	Wigan
459	Warrington	459	Warrington
460	Leigh	460	Leigh
461	Bolton	461	Bolton
462	Bury	462	Bury
463	Barton upon Irwell	463	Barton upon Irwell
464	Chorlton	464	Chorlton
465	Salford	465	Salford
466	Manchester	466	Manchester
467	Prestwich	467	Prestwich
468	Ashton under Lyne	468	Ashton under Lyne
469	Oldham	469	Oldham
470	Rochdale	470	Rochdale
471	Haslingden	471	Haslingden
472	Burnley	472	Burnley
474	Blackburn	474	Blackburn
475	Chorley	475	Chorley
476	Preston	476	Preston
477	Fylde	477	Fylde
479	Lancaster	479	Lancaster
481	Ulverston	481	Ulverston
482	Barrow in Furness	482	Barrow in Furness
491	Wharfedale	491	Wharfedale
492	Keighley	492	Keighley
493	Todmorden	493	Todmorden
494	Saddleworth	494	Saddleworth
495	Huddersfield	495	Huddersfield
496	Halifax	496	Halifax
497	Bradford	497	Bradford
498	Hunslet	498	Hunslet
499	Holbeck	499	Holbeck

1881 RD No	Place	1891 RD No	Place
500	Bramley	500	Bramley
501	Leeds	501	Leeds
502	Dewsbury	502	Dewsbury
503	Wakefield	503	Wakefield
504	Pontefract	504	Pontefract
506	Barnsley	506	Barnsley
507	Wortley	507	Wortley
508	Ecclesall Bierlow	508	Ecclesall Bierlow
509	Sheffield	509	Sheffield
510	Rotherham	510	Rotherham
511	Doncaster	511	Doncaster
516	York	516	York
520	Sculcoates	520	Sculcoates
521	Hull	521	Hull
526	Scarborough	526	Scarborough
533	Guisborough	533	Guisborough
534	Middlesbrough	534	Middlesbrough
542	Darlington	542	Darlington
543	Stockton	543	Stockton
544	Hartlepool	544	Hartlepool
545	Auckland	545	Auckland
548	Lanchester	548	Lanchester
549	Durham	549	Durham
550	Easington	550	Easington
552	Chester le Street	552	Chester le Street
553	Sunderland	553	Sunderland
554	South Shields	554	South Shields
555	Gateshead	555	Gateshead
556	Newcastle upon Tyne	556	Newcastle upon Tyne
557	Tynemouth	557	Tynemouth
562	Morpeth	562	Morpeth
572	Carlisle	572	Carlisle
574	Cockermouth	574	Cockermouth
575	Whitehaven	575	Whitehaven
579	Kendal	579	Kendal

1881		1891	
RD No	Place	RD No	Place
583	Bedwellty	583	Bedwellty
584	Pontypool	584	Pontypool
585	Newport	585	Newport
586	Cardiff	586	Cardiff
587	Pontypridd	587	Pontypridd
588	Merthyr Tydfil	588	Merthyr Tydfil
589	Bridgend	589	Bridgend
590	Neath	590	Neath
592	Swansea	592	Swansea
594	Llanelly	594	Llanelly
617	Holywell	617	Holywell
618	Wrexham	618	Wrexham
627	Caernarfon	627	Caernarfon
900	Jersey	900	Jersey

APPENDIX 10 PLACES STREET INDEXED IN PART

(available on officer's desk only)

1841	1851	1861	1871	1881
Barnet	Bedford	Barnet	Barnet	Ashby de la Zouche
Barton upon Irwell	Biggleswade	Bedford	Bedford	Dunstable
Bedford	Burnley	Dewsbury	Dunstable	Finedon
Bramley	Cheadle	Dunstable	Horsham	Hereford
Bradford	Colchester	Hartlepool	Isle of Wight	Horsham
Brentford	Congleton	Horsham	Leighton Buzzard	Kettering
Derby	Coppenhall	Hull	Lowestoft	Leighton Buzzard
Dewsbury	Dover	Isle of Wight	Luton	Loughborough
Dunstable	Hereford	Leighton Buzzard	Petworth	Lowestoft
Ecclesall Bierlow	Horsham	Lowestoft	Salisbury	Luton
Edmonton	Knutsford	Luton	Stamford	Petworth
Gloucester	Leamington	Petworth	Stapleton	Salisbury
Hendon	Leominster	Pontypridd	Walsall	Stapleton
Horsham	Lowestoft	Salisbury		
Leighton Buzzard	Melton Mowbray	Sculcoates		
Lowestoft	Petworth	Stamford		
Luton	Radford	Stapleton		
Maidstone	Runcorn	Tewkesbury		
Petworth	Stapleton	Thanet		
Plymouth		Walsall		
Sculcoates				
Stapleton				
Walsall				
Wolverhampton				

APPENDIX 11   BIBLIOGRAPHY

E J Higgs, *Making Sense of the Census: The Manuscript Returns for England and Wales, 1801-1901,* HMSO, 1989.

E J Higgs, *A Clearer Sense of the Census,* PRO Handbook 28, HMSO 1996.

Susan Lumas, *An Introduction to...The Census Returns of England and Wales,* FFHS, 1992.

Ray Wiggins, *St Catherine's House Districts,* privately printed, Northwood, no date.

J S W Gibson, *Census Returns 1841-1881 on Microfilm: A Directory to Local Holdings,* FFHS.

J S W Gibson and Colin Chapman, *Census Indexes and Indexing,* FFHS, 1983.

J S W Gibson and M Medlycott, *Local Census Listings 1522-1930, Holdings in the British Isles* , FFHS.

J S W Gibson, *Marriage, Census and other Indexes for Family Historians,* FFHS.

John M Boreham, *The Census and How to Use it,* Essex Society for Family History, 1982.

Andrew Todd, *Basic Sources for Family History: Back to the early 1880s,* Bury, Lancs, 3rd edn, 1994.

C R Chapman, *Pre 1841 Censuses and Population Listings,* Lockin Publishing, 1991.

Alan Godfrey, *Old Ordnance Survey Maps,* Gateshead, various dates.

George Pelling, *Beginning Your Family History,* 6th edn, FFHS, 1995.

M E Bryant Rosier, *Index to Census Registration Districts,* FFHS, 1990.

Frederick Engels, *The Condition of the Working Class in England,* Chapter III, p 30, ed W O Henderson and W H Chaloner, 2nd edn, Chapter III, p 30, Basil Blackwell, 1971.

Gordon Johnson, *Census Records for Scottish Families,* Association of Scottish Family History Societies, Aberdeen, 1990.

Heraldic Artists Ltd, *Handbook on Irish Genealogy,* Heraldic Artists Ltd, 1978.

Donald F Begley, *Irish Genealogy: A Record Finder,* Heraldic Artists Ltd, 1981.

People and Places in the Victorian Census: a review and bibliography of publications based substantially on the manuscript Census Enumerators' Books 1841-1911. Dennis Mills and Carol Pearce (comp), Institute of British Geographers, Historical Geography Research Series No 23, November 1989.

The Phillimore Atlas and Index of Parish Registers, ed Cecil R Humphery-Smith, Phillimore, 2nd edn, 1996.

Population of Each County of Great Britain: 1841, (sessional papers I, House of Commons, Vol II, paper no 52, 277).

Population Tables I: Numbers of the inhabitants: Vol I: 1852-1853, (sessional papers, House of Commons, Vol LXXXV, paper no 1631).

Population Tables I: Numbers of the inhabitants: Vol II: 1852-1853, (sessional papers, House of Commons, Vol LXXXVI, paper no 1632.

Population Tables I: Numbers and Distribution of the People: 1862, (sessional papers, House of Commons, Vol L, paper no 3056).

Population Tables: Area, Houses and Inhabitants: Vol I, Counties: 1872, (sessional papers, House of Commons, Vol LXVI, paper no c.671-I, Part I).

Population Tables: Area, Houses and Inhabitants: Vol II, Registration or Union Counties: 1872 (sessional papers, House of Commons, Vol LXVI, paper no c.676-I, Part II, 1).

Population Tables: Area, Houses and Population: Counties: 1883 (sessional papers, House of Commons, Vol LXXVIII, paper no c.3562, 1).

Population Tables: Registration Counties: 1883 (sessional papers, House of Commons, Vol LXXIX, paper no c.3563, 1).